# Build-It Book
# of
# Car Electronics

by

**Rudolf F. Graf**

**&**

**George J. Whalen**

Howard W. Sams & Co., Inc.
4300 WEST 62ND ST. INDIANAPOLIS, INDIANA 46268 USA

# Preface

Electronics is the car-owner's best friend! It brings precision and reliability to the tasks of ignition and battery-voltage regulation in all late-model cars. And, electronics has added new dimensions to care-borne entertainment, far enhanced driving pleasure, as well as provided vital communications for the stranded traveler whose car has broken down.

Yet, with all these improvements, there are still many more ways that electronics can enlarge the convenience of driving, give you a maintenance "edge" to keep costs in check, and add to the security of ownership of your prized vehicle. That is the subject and purpose of this book. Gathered here are a number of projects you can enjoy building and using for years to come. Each serves a worthwhile purpose and may be just what you have been looking for to help you get the most enjoyment out of your car or recreational vehicle.

While you build the projects we have included in this book for a purpose, you will also find your experience growing in the details of applying electronics to the harsh environment of motor vehicles. Remember that a good part of every car's lifetime is spent in chilling cold or baking heat, and that severe transients are common even on electronically regulated automotive 12-volt power sources. Each project described in this book has been tested and optimized for the car environment. Given care and attention to detail in construction, each project should reward you with a large measure of satisfaction and enjoyment in use.

Many of the projects described here are the result of experience gathered in connection with two of our other Sams publications: *Automotive Electronics* and *Solid-State Ignition Systems*. We are indeed grateful to the personnel of Howard W. Sams & Co., Inc., and to the staffs of *Popular Mechanics, Popular Science, Radio-Electronics,* and *Mechanix Illustrated* magazines, all of whom aided in the preparation of this work. We are also indebted to Mr. Charles Cimilluca for his thoughtful and worthwhile comments on this work, and we owe considerable gratitude to Mrs. John J. Dillon for her meritorious effort in preparing the typed manuscript, and to Michael Zarembski and Leonard Haber for their manifest expertise in the photolab.

Here, then, is the *Build-It Book of Car Electronics*. We hope you will use and enjoy it.

Rudolf F. Graf
George J. Whalen

*To David—driving hard into tomorrow*

# Contents

# 1

# AUDIO TACH

Here is an instrument that will help you get top-notch efficiency from your car engine. You can use it to measure rpm for accurate tune-up, timing, idle, and fuel-mixture adjustments. You can diagnose faulty automatic choke operation, slippage in automatic transmissions and clutch assemblies, and excessive fuel consumption due to improper carburetor settings. But, more than this, you can use the Audio Tach on the highway to "program" gear shifting for maximum performance or to warn when engine "over-rev" is approaching.

The Audio Tach (Fig. 1-1) measures engine rpm by counting ignition pulses at the breaker points and displaying its count on a meter that is calibrated in rpm. Apart from this visual display, the Audio Tach has a built-in audible alarm, which can be set to "sound off" when a specific rpm is reached! This audible-alarm feature lets you drive with your eyes on the road, rather than "glued" to the tach.

The Audio Tach features a full-scale measurement capability of 8000 rpm, making it adaptable for use with any 2-, 3-, 4-, 6-, or 8-cylinder engine. It works equally well with two-cycle or four-cycle engines, having either conventional or magneto-type ignition systems. Its layout is not critical, but care must be exercised to use *only* the components specified in the parts list.

The Audio Tach is housed in an inexpensive Bakelite instrument case, measuring 6¼ inches × 3¹¹⁄₁₆ inches × 2 inches. All major components are contained on a sheet of perforated phenolic board, measuring 4¾ inches × 3 inches. "Sandwich" construction methods are used to make a compact assembly. The meter, switches, and 2-inch-diameter loudspeaker are installed on a sheet of perforated metal (or perforated phenolic board) cut to exactly 6 inches × 3 inches in order to fit the panel opening of the Bakelite case. The wired component board mounts to the back of the meter by means of the two meter terminal screws. No other supports or hardware is needed. Leads from the component board run to the panel-mounted parts and to a three-terminal barrier-type strip on the back of the case. These terminals are connected to your engine's breaker points and to the positive and negative terminals of a 12-volt dc source, as described later.

Fig. 1-1. The Audio Tach.

## HOW IT WORKS

The schematic of the Audio Tach is shown in Fig. 1-2. The unit consists of two major sections: the *pulse-rate tachometer* and the *audible alarm*.

The pulse-rate tachometer consists of a monostable multivibrator (Q1, Q2) driving a milliammeter, M1. The monostable circuit is like a spring-loaded switch. When triggered by a pulse, it flips to the "on" state and remains there for a specific

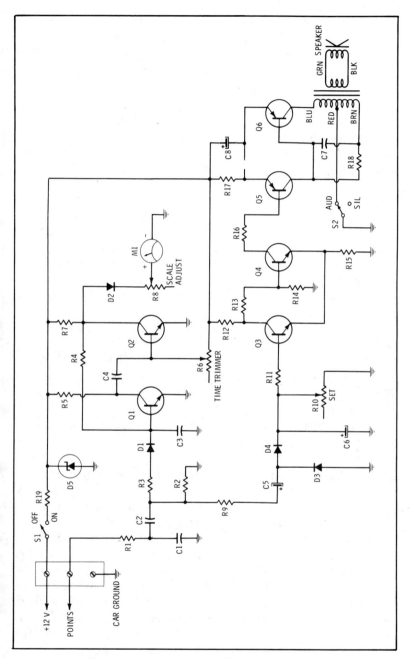

**Fig. 1-2. Schematic diagram for the Audio Tach.**

9

time, then resets itself automatically. In this application, the monostable circuit generates a series of pulses that are identical in level and duration, even though the pulses produced by the engine breaker points vary in duration with changing speed. Ringing and overshoots in the input pulses are eliminated by a filtering and clipping network (R1, C1, C2, R2, R3, D1, and C3) at the base of Q1. Transistor Q1 is normally off (nonconducting), and transistor Q2 is normally on (conducting). Each input pulse from the breaker points drives Q1 into conduction, supplying a pulse through capacitor C4 to the base of Q2, which drives Q2 off. Transistor Q2 remains off until C4 has discharged through time-trimmer potentiometer R6. During this interval, Q1 is held on by a positive voltage supplied to its base through resistor R4. When C4 is fully discharged, Q2 reverts to its normal on state. The loss of positive voltage at the collector of Q2 causes Q1 to be switched off until the next breaker-point input pulse occurs. Meter M1 is connected as a dc voltmeter in series with diode D2 and scale-adjust potentiometer R8. Each time Q2 is switched off, a voltage appears across M1, causing the pointer to deflect. The rapid on-off switching of Q2 results in a pulse voltage at the collector of Q2 that is directly proportional to rpm. The meter acts to integrate these pulses into a fairly steady reading. Diode D2 eliminates the slight saturation voltage present at the collector of Q2 when it is on, improving meter accuracy.

The audible alarm section of the Audio Tach consists of an integrator (D3, D4, C6), a Schmitt-trigger voltage-level detector (Q3, Q4), a transistor switch (Q5), and an audio oscillator (Q6). The integrator is connected to the input filter network and receives the input pulses from the ignition breaker points through capacitor C5. Diode D4 passes the positive portions of each pulse, while D3 clips off negative excursions. Each positive pulse of current passed by D4 charges capacitor C6 in "steps," increasing the voltage across C6 in proportion to engine rpm. Panel-mounted SET potentiometer R10 is in parallel with C6, forming an RC time-constant network. The setting of R10 determines how quickly C6 will reach a given charge. Therefore, R10 can be precisely set so that a specific pulse frequency is required to enable C6 to reach the required charge level. The charge developed across C6 is applied to the base-emitter junction of Q3 through resistor R11. Transistors

Q3 and Q4 comprise a modified Schmitt trigger acting as a voltage-level detector. This circuit is normally inactive until the voltage applied to its input reaches a specified level. At that point, the circuit switches on and remains on until the voltage decreases below the trigger level. Normally, Q3 is off and Q4 is on. Collector current for Q4 is supplied through the emitter-base junction of pnp transistor switch Q5 and resistor R16. As long as Q4 is on, Q5 is also held on, shunting the emitter-base junction of audio oscillator Q6. Hence, the audio oscillator stage is squelched under normal conditions. However, when engine rpm reaches a desired level, the voltage across C6 and R10 triggers transistor Q3 on, regeneratively turning off transistor Q4. When Q4 turns off, Q5 is also turned off, and its emitter-collector resistance jumps to a high value. When this happens, Q6 is biased on and commences to oscillate due to the feedback provided to its base through transformer T1. RC network C7-R18 in the base circuit of Q6 sets the oscillation frequency in the range of 500 to 600 Hz. Emitter-current limiting is provided by resistor R17, which is bypassed for audio frequencies by capacitor C8. Transistor Q6 delivers an audio signal at a level of approximately 50 milliwatts to speaker SK1 through the 8-ohm secondary winding of transformer T1.

The tone output from the speaker alerts the driver that the desired rpm level has been reached. Shifting to a higher gear or decelerating will result in lower engine rpm. When the breaker-point input pulses no longer reach the threshold level of the Schmitt trigger, the circuit reverts to its normal state. Transistor Q5 is turned on again and the audio oscillator, Q6, is biased off.

Power for operation of the Audio Tach is obtained from the 12-volt car battery or from an external 12-volt battery. To ensure accuracy, voltages supplied to the monostable multivibrator and Schmitt trigger are regulated at 9.1-volts dc by zener diode D5, in conjunction with resistor R19.

## CONSTRUCTION

Assembly of the Audio Tach is fairly straightforward. If you wish to duplicate the authors' version, follow the layout shown in Fig. 1-3. Cut the front panel from perforated sheet metal or phenolic board material. The $2\%_{16}$-inch-diameter hole for meter M1 can be cut by using a "nibbling" tool. Holes for the two switches and SET potentiometer can be drilled and reamed to size. The 2-inch-diameter loudspeaker requires two holes spaced diagonally 2½ inches apart.

When you have cut and drilled the panel, install the SET control, switches, and speaker. Next, cut the phenolic component board to size and place it on the back of meter M1 so that it rests on the meter terminals. Mark the terminal hole locations on the board and then locate the holes for transformer T1 to prevent interference in assembly later.

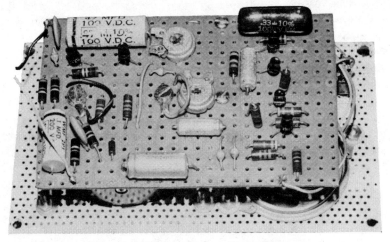

Fig. 1-3. Audio-Tach component board.

You can now proceed to assemble components on the component board as shown in Fig. 1-3. Wiring is point to point, and no special precautions need to be observed other than to take care to install the electrolytic capacitors, diodes, and transistors with correct polarity.

When you have finished the wiring, paint the front panel and apply decals for a finished appearance. Next, install the new rpm calibration scale on the face of meter M1. Open the meter by removing the four tiny Phillips-head screws on the back of the meter case. Remove the cover and gently unthread the two screws securing the meter face to the movement. Delicately remove the face, being careful not to damage the meter pointer. A full-size rpm calibration scale (Fig. 1-4) is provided. It can be photocopied and secured over the existing scale by using a drop or two of rubber cement. When it is dry, reinstall the meter face and reassemble the meter. You can now install the meter in the front panel of the Audio Tach.

Speaker SK1 is held in place by two solder lugs secured with screws, nuts, and washers. The lugs bear against the metal rim of the speaker, holding it securely against the panel. Referring to the schematic in Fig. 1-2, wire the panel-mounted components to the assembled component board. Next, assemble terminal strip TS1 to the rear of the Bakelite case. Drill two holes for mounting the terminal strip and drill three holes opposite the three terminals for connection of leads. Drill the holes carefully to avoid chipping the case. Install the terminal strip and connect one end of a wire lead under each terminal screw. Pass these leads through the holes in the case and connect them to switch S1, resistor R1, and the ground bus. When these steps are completed, make a thorough final check of the wiring and assembly to make certain that there are no wiring errors. When you have done this, you are ready to calibrate your Audio Tach.

**RPM**
**x 1000**

**Fig. 1-4. Meter scale for Audio Tach.**

### CALIBRATION

Your completed Audio Tach must be calibrated for the type of engine with which it will be used. Two calibration methods are given: the first method gives the most accuracy but requires test gear you may not have; the second method yields an instrument of somewhat less accuracy but requires little in the way of test gear. Choose the method that best suits your circumstances.

The first calibration method requires an audio generator capable of producing sine or square waves in the frequency range of 30 to 1200 Hz. If you do not have such a generator, you can take your Audio Tach to a local television or hi-fi service shop that does and have them calibrate it for you. Table 1-1 lists the ignition pulse rates of most common two-cycle and four-cycle engines, in 1000-rpm steps from 1000 to 8000 rpm. The audio generator simulates the ignition breaker-point pulses for bench calibration. You will also need a 12-volt dc source to power the Audio Tach. Two 6-volt lantern batteries connected in series make an ideal supply. Connect the generator and battery supply to the Audio Tach as shown in Fig. 1-5.

### Table 1-1. Ignition Pulse Rate Versus RPM for Common Engine Types

| | Ignition Breaker-Point Pulses per Second | | | | | | | |
|---|---|---|---|---|---|---|---|---|
| Engine Type | Rpm 1000 | 2000 | 3000 | 4000 | 5000 | 6000 | 7000 | 8000 |
| 4-cylinder, 4-cycle | 33 | 66 | 100 | 133 | 166 | 200 | 233 | 266 |
| 6-cylinder, 4-cycle | 50 | 100 | 150 | 200 | 250 | 300 | 350 | 400 |
| 8-cylinder, 4-cycle | 66 | 132 | 200 | 266 | 332 | 400 | 466 | 532 |
| 2-cylinder, 2-cycle (Magneto ignition) | 33 | 66 | 100 | 133 | 166 | 200 | 233 | 266 |
| 3-cylinder, 2-cycle | 50 | 100 | 150 | 200 | 250 | 300 | 350 | 400 |
| 4-cylinder, 2-cycle | 66 | 132 | 200 | 266 | 332 | 400 | 466 | 532 |
| 6-cylinder, 2-cycle | 100 | 200 | 300 | 400 | 500 | 600 | 700 | 800 |
| 8-cylinder, 2-cycle | 132 | 264 | 400 | 532 | 664 | 800 | 932 | 1064 |

Next, referring to the data given in Table 1-1, set the generator frequency to the ignition pulse rate corresponding to 8000 rpm for your engine type. Set the generator output to give at least 8 volts of signal input to the Audio Tach. Now, set switch S1 to the ON position and observe the deflection of meter M1. Adjust time-trimmer potentiometer R6 until M1 just indicates 8000 rpm. Then, set the generator to the frequency corresponding to 1000 rpm and observe the Audio Tach reading. If the meter pointer lies above or below the mark that indicates 1000, set scale-adjust potentiometer R8 so that the meter indicates correctly. Recheck at the frequency corresponding to 8000 rpm and readjust time-trimmer R6 if necessary.

To check the audible-alarm portion of the circuit, set the generator to the frequency corresponding to 5000 rpm for your engine type, and adjust the SET potentiometer (R10) until the

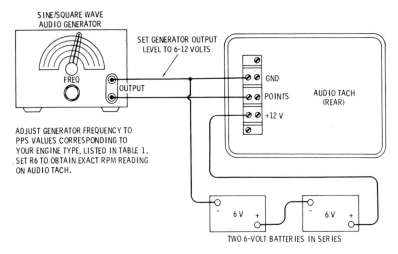

**Fig. 1-5. Preferred calibration setup for Audio Tach using an audio generator.**

audio oscillator sounds. Decrease the generator frequency setting until the audio oscillator is silenced; then run it back up to the previous setting. As the Audio Tach meter reaches the 5000-rpm mark, the audio oscillator should trigger again. Upon completion of this procedure, the Audio Tach may be assembled into its case and installed in your car.

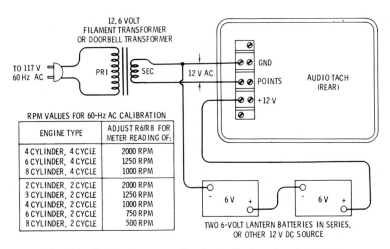

**Fig. 1-6. Calibration setup for Audio Tach using the 60-Hz ac-line frequency.**

The second calibration method enables you to do a fair job of setting up your Audio Tach by using the test setup in Fig. 1-6 instead of an audio generator. In this method, the 60-Hz frequency of the ac power line is used to simulate ignition pulses. While the accuracy of this method is not as precise as the previous method, it is sufficient for an instrument that will be used casually.

Make the setup as shown in Fig. 1-6 and connect the transformer primary to a 117-volt, 60-Hz ac line. Rotate scale-adjust potentiometer R8 for maximum deflection of M1. Do not allow the meter to slam against the pin; just set it for maximum deflection, or to 8000 rpm, if possible. Now, adjust time-trimmer potentiometer R6 for the meter rpm reading corresponding to your engine type, as shown in Fig. 1-6. If necessary, set R8 in conjunction with R6 to get an exact reading.

After you have made this adjustment, you can proceed to hook up the Audio Tach to your engine.

## HOOKING IT UP

Connecting the Audio Tach to most engines is simple. For conventional ignition systems, connect a lead between the POINTS terminal on terminal-strip TS1 and the (−) terminal of the engine ignition coil, as shown in Fig. 1-7. Connect the GND terminal of TS1 to any convenient ground screw on the chassis or the engine block. Attach the lead from the +12-V terminal of TS1 to any convenient terminal on the auto fuseblock (usually located under the dash on the driver's side). The fused instrument or accessory terminals are ideal for this connection. If you wish to make a permanent installation in an auto, truck, or boat, you need only run the POINTS lead into the engine compartment. The GND and +12-V leads can be connected in the driving compartment. (An ideal feedthrough point for the POINTS lead is the grommeted speedometer hole, usually located on the firewall just below the dashboard on the driver's side of most cars.) Where an electronic ignition system is used, connect to the + terminal of the ignition coil, or follow the manufacturer's hookup that is recommended for a tachometer.

For operation with magneto-type ignition systems (used in outboard motors, tractors, and motorcycles), you will have to

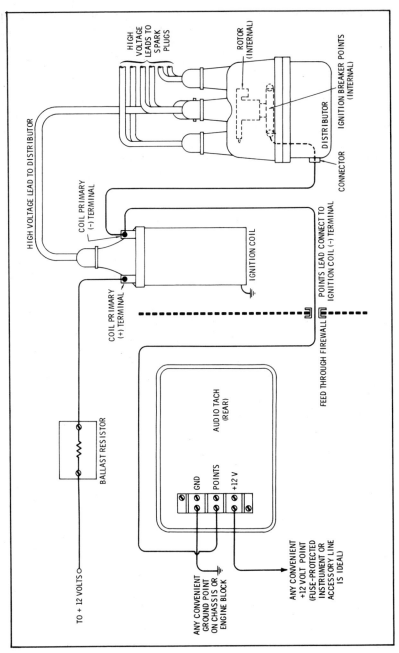

**Fig.1-7. Audio-Tach hookup for a conventional ignition system.**

make some provision for power to operate the Audio Tach. Two 6-volt lantern batteries connected in series make a long-life 12-volt supply that can be stashed away in any convenient location. The batteries can be connected by reasonable-length leads to the +12-V and GND terminals of the Audio Tach.

Magneto ignition systems use a built-in generator instead of the battery found in conventional ignition systems. This built-in generator develops a moderate dc voltage that is interrupted by the ignition breaker points and stepped up to spark-plug firing potential through a secondary coil surrounding the generator coil. In most engines employing magneto ignition, you can attach a lead directly to the ungrounded breaker-point terminal (the terminal connected to the condenser lead) and bring it out to the Audio Tach.

In Chrysler outboard engines, the engineers have thoughtfully provided a tachometer lead (color-coded white) as part of the standard harness assembly. This lead comes directly from the breaker points and should be connected to the POINTS terminal on the Audio Tach.

If you have any doubts about connecting the Audio Tach to your ignition system, consult your engine overhaul manual or the service department of a local dealer agency for details.

## USING THE AUDIO TACH

You will find the Audio Tach a real help in tuning up your car's engine. Antipollution devices call for timing and carburetion adjustments to be made at specific engine rpm. You can set and hold rpm exactly as specified by using the Audio Tach meter. Also, you can check operation of your engine's automatic choke. Engine rpm should reduce with warm-up, and the Audio Tach meter will show this far more accurately than you can detect by ear. Faulty ignition components will also show up on the Audio Tach meter. Erratic meter readings may indicate bouncing points, a defective coil or condenser, or excessive wear in the distributor cam shaft. Automatic transmissions can also be checked with the Audio Tach. Since shift points of the transmission are directly related to engine rpm, slippage in the transmission can be detected by watching the meter pointer and seeing if it exceeds the shift rpm specified by the manufacturer. Engine idle speed is another critical adjustment in which the Audio Tach can help a lot. If your engine idles too slow, it may stall easily. An idle speed that is too fast means wasted fuel, excessive strain on the transmission and brakes, and the annoyance of excessive "creep." You can precisely set idle speed with the Audio Tach and, by teaming it up with a vacuum gauge, you can make a professional fuel-mixture adjustment for all-around best performance and economy.

The audible-alarm feature of the Audio Tach can be used anytime you want an indication of the meter reading but cannot divert your attention to watch it. This is especially helpful at night, when your eyes should not leave the road, even for an instant. Drivers of cars with manual transmissions gain extra benefits from the Audio Tach. If you know the manufacturer's specified rpm for maximum torque output from your engine, you can set the Audio Tach to sound when that rpm is reached. You can then shift and ride the rpm up to maximum torque again all without once taking your eyes off the road ahead!

For "over-rev" protection, just set the audible alarm to sound about 500 rpm below the engine red-line rpm. This setting will guarantee your being warned in the event that rpm is becoming excessive.

## Table 1-2. Audio Tach Parts List

C1, C3—.01-$\mu$F, 600-V dc disc capacitor
C2—.1-$\mu$F, 200-V dc capacitor
C4—.47-$\mu$F, 100-V dc capacitor
C5—10-$\mu$F, 100-V dc electrolytic capacitor
C6, C8—10-$\mu$F, 25-V dc electrolytic capacitor
C7—.33-$\mu$F, 100-V dc capacitor
D1 to D4—general-purpose silicon diode type 1N5060
D5—9.1-V, 1-W zener diode (Motorola HEP Z0412 or equiv)
M1—0–1 milliampere meter (Lafayette 99F50874 or equiv)
Q1, Q2—npn transistor, type 2N3414 or equiv
Q3, Q4—npn transistor, type 2N5172 or equiv
Q5, Q6—pnp transistor, type 2N2907 or equiv
R1, R2, R3, R9, R11—1000-ohm, ½-W ±10% resistor
R4—15,000-ohm, ½-W ±10% resistor
R5—1200-ohm, ½-W ±10% resistor
R6, R8—10,000-ohm potentiometer (Mallory type MTC-14L4 or equiv)
R7—820-ohm, ½-W ±10% resistor
R10—25,000-ohm potentiometer (IRC type Q11-120 or equiv)
R12, R16—4700-ohm, ½-W ±10% resistor
R13—2200-ohm, ½-W ±10% resistor
R14—6800-ohm, ½-W ±10% resistor
R15—150-ohm, ½-W ±10% resistor
R17—100-ohm, ½-W ±10% resistor
R18—7500-ohm, ½-W ±10% resistor
R19—220-ohm, ½-W ±10% resistor
S1, S2—miniature spdt toggle switch (Alcoswitch type MST-105D or equiv)
SK1—2-inch-diameter, 0.25-W, 8-ohm speaker
T1—transistor output transformer, 1000-ohm ct primary, 8-ohm secondary
  (Argonne type AR-137 or equiv)
TS1—three-terminal barrier strip (Cinch-Jones type 3-140 or equiv)
Misc—Instrument case, 6¼″ × 3¾″ × 2″ (Radio Shack 270-627 or
  equiv); perforated panel, 4¾″ × 3″ perforated phenolic component
  board; knob; hookup wire; solder.

# 2

# BATTERY-CONDITION CHECKER

Each of us faces a "moment of truth" when we turn the key in the ignition switch for the morning start-up. The car battery is given a rigorous exam by the voracious starting motor. Battery current of nearly 400 amperes is needed to crank a cold, high-compression engine off dead center. If the battery passes, you start; if not, you sit and listen to the disheartening "clickety-click-click" of the solenoid as it vainly makes and breaks the circuit to the deceased battery.

Not all of us are as sensitive as we should be to the somewhat subtle indications of a failing battery. It takes a keenly developed sense of hearing to detect a slower-than-normal cranking speed, a slight hesitation in the cranking action, or a somewhat longer-than-usual cranking period. The instruments used to indicate the condition of the electrical system in most vehicles are barely any help, either. The widely misunderstood charging ammeter gives ambiguous indications. It reads zero-center for a fully charged battery—but you get the *same* zero indication if the alternator belt is slipping or the regulator has failed. The "idiot light" detects only complete failure of the charging system; it cannot determine the battery's capacity to deliver energy.

The 12-volt lead-acid storage battery that powers the starting system of an automobile is often subjected to harsh use. Low temperature extremes sap the battery's capacity, and frequent start-ups, little actual driving, or defects in the charging system can keep it constantly undercharged. It is little wonder that *battery failure* ranks so high on the list of problems that car owners suffer.

Yet, battery failure does not occur unannounced. The conditions that will lead to a "no-start" if left unchecked are usually detectable days or even weeks in advance. All that is needed is the *means* of detecting them—*while there is still time to do something about them!*

Engineers have long recognized that an accurate test of the condition of a lead-acid battery can be made by measuring the voltage across its terminals *while the battery is actually supplying current to a load*. It is generally agreed that the terminal voltage of a 12-volt automotive battery should not fall below 9.2 volts when initially loaded by the starting motor. The *automatic battery-condition checker* shown in Fig. 2-1

Fig. 2-1. Battery-condition checker installed in cigarette-lighter socket.

allows the driver, while comfortably seated, to check his battery in seconds as part of the normal morning start-up routine.

The complete circuit is contained in a cigarette-lighter accessory plug, usually used to tap power for accessories (lights, etc) from the vehicle's cigarette-lighter socket. The plug body has two terminals—a blunt positive terminal at the tip and a flat negative terminal along the side. An indicator lamp is mounted at the rear end of the plug body. The checker is designed to slide into the cigarette-lighter socket and thereby establish contact with the battery through the vehicle wiring.

A simple voltage-sensitive switching circuit is incorporated entirely into the body of the checker. This circuit is designed to discriminate between the terminal voltage under load that represents a battery in good condition and the voltage that represents a discharged or deteriorated battery.

## HOW IT WORKS

The checker is inserted into the cigarette-lighter socket. Immediately, the lamp glows and remains on. The driver now cranks and starts the engine while observing the checker lamp. Should the lamp extinguish during cranking, the voltage across the battery has dropped *below* the acceptable norm for an average battery under the load imposed by the starting motor. Should the lamp go out, even if the car starts, trouble may be at hand. Of course, if the battery is good, the lamp remains glowing during the entire cranking interval. After starting, you simply unplug the checker and store it in the glove compartment. Although a daily check is informative, a weekly check should be adequate to detect the onset of battery deterioration.

The input circuit (as shown in Fig. 2-2) comprises a silicon diode and a zener diode. Diode D1 has an approximate (but virtually constant) turn-on voltage of 0.6 volt. The zener diode, D2, has an avalanche voltage of 7.5 volts (also constant). Thus, current has no path through the series diodes until the

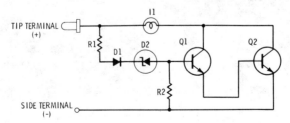

**Fig. 2-2. Battery-condition checker schematic.**

potential difference is greater than 8.1 volts. The output voltage at the junction of D2 and R2 is applied to transistor Q1 and Q2, which are connected as a Darlington transistor switch. This compound transistor does not conduct until the potential difference between its base and emitter exceeds 1.2 volts. Only then does this transistor combination act as a closed switch so that current may flow through indicator lamp I1. This means that the voltage which *must* be present at the input of Q1 cannot be *less* than 9.3 volts (0.6 V + 7.5 V + 1.2 V), if the lamp is to be switched on. With an input voltage above 9.3 volts, the circuit functions as it would at 9.3 volts (lamp on). During cranking, if the battery voltage falls *below* 9.3 volts, forward bias is removed from the base of Q1 and the Darlington switch is turned off. Thus, the lamp goes out, and you have an indication that the battery has failed under load!

There are no controls, and indicator interpretation is simple. If the battery is good, the lamp is on; if the battery is bad, the lamp is off. The automatic battery-condition checker is readily transferred from car to car, as well as to a boat or snowmobile.

## CONSTRUCTION

The seven components plus indicator light that make up the circuit all fit snugly *inside* a standard cigarette-lighter accessory plug (Figs. 2-3 and 2-4). First, drill out the rivet that holds the two halves of the plug together and remove the small separating struts at the rear of the plug. Next, hold the two halves of the plug firmly together and drill (or file) a $\frac{5}{16}$-inch-diameter hole to a depth of $\frac{3}{8}$ inch for the pilot light.

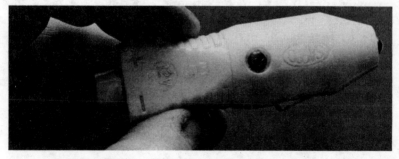

Fig. 2-3. Assembled battery-condition checker.

The pilot-light assembly is $^{15}/_{16}$ inch long and must be shortened to fit in the hole. Cut away $^{3}/_{16}$ inch for an overall length of $^{3}/_{4}$ inch. To make room for the pilot-light assembly, the two metal contact strips are bent around the two plastic posts which support them.

Wire the transistors, diodes, and resistors inside the plug as shown in Fig. 2-4. The whole assembly nestles nicely inside

Fig. 2-4. Internal view of battery-condition checker showing component layout.

one half of the plug after some of the struts are removed with a pair of long-nose pliers. Be careful that none of the connections short. To prevent this, we used a few small pieces of clear plastic separators cut from the blister package of the accessory plug. The pilot-light assembly can be held in place with a dab of clear cement. A $^{3}/_{4}$-inch-long screw and nut replace the rivet and hold the two halves firmly together. Neither the screw nor the nut may extend beyond the body of the plug. If they do, the plug will not fit into the cigarette-lighter socket.

## Table 2-1. Battery-Condition Checker Parts List

D1—general-purpose silicon diode (Motorola HEP R0052 or equiv)
D2—7.5V, 1-W ±5% zener diode (Mallory ZB7.5B or equiv)
Q1, Q2—npn silicon transistor, type 2N5376 or equiv
R1—120-ohm, ½-W ±20% resistor*
R2—4700-ohm, ½-W ±20% resistor*
I1—12-V, 150-mA max incandescent pilot light (Industrial Devices 2990D1-
   12V or equiv)
Cigarette-lighter accessory plug (Radio Shack 274-331 or equiv)
* If available, use ¼-watt resistors for easier fit.

# 3

# BRAKE-LIGHT MONITOR

Reliable as automotive lamps are, they can *still* burn out at unexpected moments. Perhaps the most dangerous failure is the loss of a rear brake light, since this type of failure robs your car of two important signalling functions: it reduces the warning to the driver behind you that your car is braking, and it sharply curtails your ability to signal a turn. Of course, the degree of severity of the failure is related to the number of lamps in your car's rear-end signaling system. If your car has only *one* stoplight for each side, a lamp failure can be an open invitation to a deadly collision!

The most insidious factor in brake-lamp failures is that the filament opens up quietly, and in a position that cannot be seen from the driver's seat. Occasionally checking the lamps at a service station with the aid of an attendant may help, but it is no guarantee that a brake lamp won't fail two minutes after you have driven away. The brake-light monitor shown in Fig. 3-1 gives you a dependable indication of whether or not your car's most vital signal lamps are functioning properly. Should any lamp become inoperative, a light will instantly flash on in the monitor to warn you of the hazardous condition.

## HOW IT WORKS

The most important part of the circuit is a tiny reed relay to which a second winding, consisting of 6 turns of No. 14

enamelled wire, has been added. As shown in Fig. 3-2, this added winding is connected in series with the lead that goes from the stoplight switch to the brake lamps, so that the full lamp current flows through this winding enroute to the lamp filaments. The lamp current produces a magnetic field that is

Fig. 3-1. Brake-light monitor.

proportional to the current required by the filaments. In the case of a two-lamp stoplight system, this current would be from 4 to 5 amperes. This rather respectable amount of current produces a fairly strong magnetic field, which is *added* to the magnetic field generated by the existing winding on relay K1. The field strength of the existing winding is adjusted

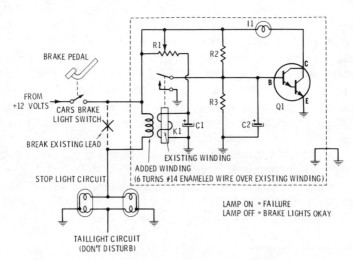

Fig. 3-2. Brake-light monitor schematic.

by R1 so that it is just sufficient to close the reed contacts. Hence, the magnetic field produced by the stoplight current flowing through the additional winding is summed with the field of the existing winding every time you step on the brakes. If any one of the lamps is inoperative (either because it is burned out or because of poor electrical contact) there will be proportionately less current through the added 6-turn winding and the reed relay will not close.

Capacitor C2 and resistor R2, together with Darlington transistor Q1, form a one-second time delay circuit. The collector Q1 is connected through indicator lamp I1 to +12 volts. At the instant that the brake pedal is depressed and +12 volts is applied to resistor R2, the delay is started. After one second, capacitor C2 is charged and transistor Q1 will turn indicator lamp I1 on *unless* the reed relay is closed. If the relay closes, the base of transistor Q1 is connected to ground and the transistor cannot turn on. As you can see, current flow corresponding to "good brake lamps" automatically disarms the circuit controlling the indicator lamp.

The directional-light circuit causes one rear lamp to flash, but the monitor delay circuit keeps the FAILURE lamp "off" during the short period of time that the stoplight circuit is opened for blinking action. If the delay circuit were not incorporated, the brake-light monitor lamp would flash every time you signalled a turn. It is possible that the directional lights will flash only for a very brief period of time; this may be the case when you have a defective flasher or use incorrect bulbs. In either case, the "off" period would be beyond normal limits. Thus, if the circuit is interrupted for more than one second, the brake-light monitor will flash regularly (or occasionally) whenever your turn signals are on, thereby warning you of a defect in your directional-light circuit.

## CONSTRUCTION

The unit is housed in a 4-inch × 2⅛-inch × 1⅝-inch aluminum minibox. As shown in Fig. 3-3, the failure indicator lamp is mounted on one face of the U-shaped channel, and the barrier terminal strip is mounted on the rear face. The left terminal on the barrier strip goes to +12 volts through the brake-light switch. The center terminal goes to the stoplights, and the third terminal goes to chassis ground. All the electronic components are mounted on one side of a 2-inch × 3½-inch piece of perf board. For ease of assembly, flea clips are used to make the connections on the perf board. The perf board is held in place by two ¾-inch screws that go through half-inch spacers that keep the board a proper distance from the chassis to prevent shorts.

## CALIBRATION

The circuit sensitivity needs to be adjusted only one time. Step on the brake pedal so that the stoplights go on. Simultaneously adjust potentiometer R1 from full resistance (lamp on) until the reed relay just closes and indicator lamp I1 goes off. To simulate lamp failure, reach into the trunk and unplug one stoplight assembly from the frame of the car, making sure it does not touch the metal body of the car. Now, when you step on the brake pedal again, the indicator light should go on after one second, signalling that the lamp circuit is not operating properly. If the indicator lamp does not go on, increase R1 slightly until the lamp just goes on. Then, reinsert

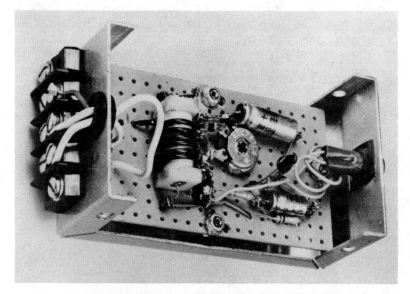

**Fig. 3-3. Internal view of brake-light monitor showing component layout.**

the stoplight assembly previously removed. Pump the brake pedal once again. This time the warning lamp should not go on, indicating that the stoplight circuit is all right. For proper operation of the monitor, it is necessary that the fields of both relay windings *aid* each other. If it is not possible to calibrate the monitor by adjusting the potentiometer, simply reverse the two lead connections to the added-turn winding so that the direction of its current flow is reversed. This will solve your problems and proper adjustment will then be possible.

### Table 3-1. Brake-Light Monitor Parts List

R1—25,000-ohm potentiometer (Mallory MTC253L4 or equiv)
R2, R3—100,000-ohm, ½-W ±10% resistor
C1—20-$\mu$F, 50-V dc electrolytic capacitor
C2—10-$\mu$F, 25-V dc electrolytic capacitor
Q1—npn silicon Darlington transistor, type 2N5306 or equiv
K1—reed relay, 12-V dc, 120-ohm coil (Magnecraft W101 MX-2)
I1—12-V pilot light (Industrial Devices 2990D1-12V or equiv)
Misc—4″ × 2⅛″ × 1⅝″ aluminum minibox (Bud CU-2102A or equiv);
    three-terminal barrier strip (Cinch-Jones type 3-140 or equiv); 2″ ×
    3½″ perf board; ½″ spacers (2); screws; flea clips

# 4

# COMPUTALARM

While you are reading this chapter, an automobile is being stolen somewhere in the United States. Every minute of every day, someone's car is driven away without the owner's knowledge. This amounts to more than 500,000 cars being stolen every year. The chances that your car will be stolen are increasing every year. Yet, only 30% of stolen cars are taken by professional car thieves. Most car theft is the work of moonlighting amateurs. Even if a car is recovered (a good number are), chances are it will be stripped-down or wrecked. Car insurance offers some relief but generally does not cover all costs, inconvenience, and loss of property or special equipment installed in your car. Build the all-electronic Computalarm shown in Fig. 4-1 for a very nominal one-time expense, and you can protect the hood, trunk, and passenger compartment of your car against assault by any thief.

Many of the automobile burglar alarm systems on the market today are either relatively expensive, difficult to install, or inadequate in their protection. Some put a prolonged and undue strain on the battery as well as on the ears and nerves of people within a block or more. Such alarms usually continue their shrieking action for a far longer period than is necessary to scare away the would-be thief or attract the attention of a policeman. Also, there is not much point to protecting the car with one of these types of alarms if it means that the battery will be exhausted when you return!

**Fig. 4-1. The Computalarm.**

This is not the case with the Computalarm. The alarm remains in action for a sufficiently long period of time to scare away the would-be thief. It then turns itself off and automatically rearms. It is ready to do its job again, without having driven all bystanders out of their minds and without having drained the battery.

The Computalarm protects as many points of entry to the car as you wish. It has several distinct operating features:

1. The circuit has a built-in, self-arming feature. The driver turns off the ignition, presses the ARM button on the Computalarm, and leaves the car. Within 20 seconds the alarm arms itself—all automatically!

2. The circuit will then detect the opening of any monitored door, the trunk lid, or the hood on the car. When triggered, the circuit latches on so that even if the door, trunk, or hood lid is closed, the circuit remains activated.

3. Once activated, the circuit remains dormant for 10 seconds. When the 10-second time delay has run out, the circuit will close the car's horn relay and sound the horn in periodic blasts (approximately 1 to 2 seconds apart) for a period of one minute. No burglar is likely to wait around that long with the alarm on. Then the Computalarm automatically shuts itself off (to save your battery) and rearms. Of course, if a door, the trunk lid, or the hood lid remains ajar, the alarm circuit retriggers and another period of horn blasts occurs.

4. The Computalarm has a "key" switch by which the driver can disarm the alarm circuit within a 10-second period after he enters the door. The key switch consists of a closed circuit jack, J1, and a mating miniature plug that is small enough to carry on your key chain (Fig. 4-2). The plug fits into a similar jack on your key chain and is merely removed from that jack and plugged into J1 on the Computalarm to disarm the alarm, so that you alone can enter the car without the horn sounding.

## HOW THE CIRCUIT OPERATES

The courtesy-light door switches are used to protect the doors, and single-pole single-throw microswitches are installed under the hood and trunk lid of the car. These switches are installed so that when a door, hood, or trunk lid is closed, the switches remain open. When any portal is opened, a switch closes and triggers the circuit. (You can also experiment with a variety of other switch types like mercury switches or acceleration-sensitive switches. Thus, if someone jostles the car or attempts to move it or jack it up to steal your wheels, the alarm circuit will be activated.)

When a switch closes, it applies a ground to one end of resistor R1, R2, or R3 at the input to transistor Q1, which is normally not conducting. When one of the resistors is grounded, Q1 turns on and the collector voltage at R9 jumps up the +12-volt level of the battery. This voltage causes zener diode D2 to conduct and develop about 2 volts across resistors R4 and R5. This voltage is sufficient to turn on SCR1 and SCR2, both of which are sensitive silicon-controlled rectifiers. When these SCRs turn on, they latch and allow current to flow through the

Fig. 4-2. Key for the Computalarm.

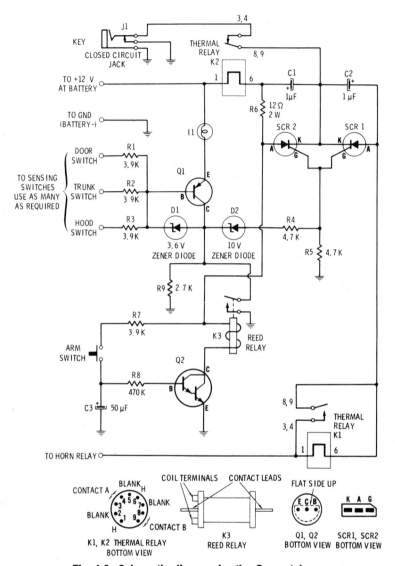

**Fig. 4-3. Schematic diagram for the Computalarm.**

heater windings of thermal relays K1 and K2. (Once an SCR has been turned on, it will continue to conduct as long as a source of current is applied to its anode and the return-path circuit remains complete.)

This is how the Computalarm latching action works. When

the heaters of relays K1 and K2 are energized, they commence to warm bimetallic contacts. Relay K1 is a normally open thermal relay, while relay K2 is a normally closed thermal relay. When energized, relay K1 will close itself within 10 seconds. Similarly, relay K2 will open within 60 seconds. The cathodes of SCR1 and SCR2 go to ground through the closed contacts of thermal relay K2 and through jack J1, which is closed whenever the plug (key) is not in it. Within 10 seconds after SCR1 is gated on, the contacts of thermal-relay K1 close. This grounds one end of the car's horn relay, causing the horns to sound. To make the horn operate in blasts, relay K1 is arranged so that when its contacts close, its heater is momentarily shorted, causing it to cool and open the bimetallic contacts. The low heater current through the horn-relay winding is not sufficient to cause the horn to blow, but as the heater warms once more, the contacts of K1 close again. The cycle repeats in a period of about every 2 seconds. While relay K1 is operating the horn circuit, the bimetallic contacts of relay K2 are receiving a constant warming from its heater.

After somewhat more than 1 minute, the contacts of relay K2 are sufficiently warm to open. This interruption causes both SCRs to commutate, which stops the horn from sounding and automatically resets the circuit.

If a door, trunk lid, or hood remains ajar, a ground will still be present on one of the resistors (R1, R2, or R3) at the base of transistor Q1, and the cycle will repeat. But if the door, trunk lid, or hood has been slammed shut the circuit will return to the standby condition when the SCRs commutate and the horn will stop sounding.

Since the Computalarm responds to a switch closure every time a door is opened, some means must be provided to allow the driver or passenger to leave the car without falsely actuating the alarm. This is the function of the delay circuit consisting of transistor Q2 and reed relay K3. Transistor Q2 is a very sensitive amplifier which can be made to operate like a switch that remains closed for a period of time and then opens by itself. The input circuit to Q2 consists of capacitor C3 and resistor R8.

When the driver and passengers want to leave the car, the driver merely waits until all passengers have left the car and closed their doors. Next, he removes the plug (key) from jack

J1 and depresses the ARM push-button switch. When he does this, the capacitor C3 in the base circuit of transistor Q2 is charged quickly to +12 volts. This turns on Q2, which pulls in the contacts of reed relay K3, grounding the collector of transistor Q1.

Indicator light I1 is now turned on to indicate that the circuit is getting ready to arm itself. After about 20 seconds, which gives the driver sufficient time to leave the car, the light goes out and the circuit is armed. The next time a door is opened, the entrant has 10 seconds in which to insert the correct size "key" into jack J1 or the alarm will sound the horn.

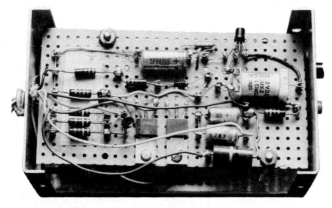

Fig. 4-4. Internal view of Computalarm showing component layout.

Construction of the Computalarm is simple. As shown in Figs. 4-4 and 4-5, all components with the exception of relays K1 and K2 are mounted on a 2½-inch × 5-inch piece of perf board. The sockets for K1 and K2 are held by screws to one side of the U-shaped portion of the aluminum minibox. The arming push button, indicator light L1, and jack J1 are mounted on the opposite side. The wires to the protective switches, the battery, the horn relay, and ground are passed through a rubber grommet.

The Computalarm can be mounted at any convenient location under the dash, or even in the glove compartment. Choose a spot in your car that is best suited for you.

In some cars, the horn may be disconnected relatively quickly because of the use of quick-disconnect cable plugs

Fig. 4-5. Internal view of Computalarm showing mounting for thermal relay K1.

that are used in most modern automobiles. To thwart any quick disconnecting, we would suggest that these leads be securely taped to the horn terminals. Better protection would be afforded by installing a sheet metal barrier to block access to horns and by using armored cable to protect the horn wiring against attack.

## Table 4-1. Computalarm Parts List

C1, C2—1-$\mu$F, 25-V dc electrolytic capacitor
C3—50-$\mu$F, 25-V dc electrolytic capacitor
D1—3.6-V, ¼-W zener diode, type 1N757A or equiv
D2—10-V, ¼-W zener diode, type 1N765 or equiv
I1—12-V, 100-mA pilot lamp (Industrial Devices 2990A1-12V or equiv)
J1—miniature closed-circuit phone jack (Switchcraft 42A or equiv)
K1—normally open, 10-second delay thermal relay (Amperite 6N010T or equiv)
K2—normally closed, 60-second delay thermal relay (Amperite 6C60T or equiv)
K3—spst, normally open, 12-V reed relay (Magnecraft W101MX-2 or equiv)
P1—miniature phone plug for jack J1
Q1—pnp silicon transistor (Motorola HEP S0012 or equiv)
Q2—npn silicon Darlington transistor, type 2N5306 or equiv
R1, R2, R3, R7—3900-ohm, ½-W ±10% resistor
R4, R5—4700-ohm, ½-W ±10% resistor
R6—120-ohm, 2-W ±10% resistor
R8—470,000-ohm, ½-W ±10% resistor
R9—2700-ohm, ½-W ±10% resistor
S1—spst, normally open push-button switch
SCR1, SCR2—silicon-controlled rectifier (General Electric type C106Y1 or equiv)
Misc—9-pin miniature tube socket for K1 and K2: 2½" × 5" perf board; 5¼" × 3" × 2⅛" aluminum minibox (Bud CU-2106A or equiv); sensing switches as required

# 5

# WINDSHIELD-WIPER
# CONTROLLER

Suppose that a light drizzle or snow is falling, or that the car ahead of you is spraying fine mist and road scum onto your windshield after a snow or rainfall. You turn on your windshield wipers, but, more often than not, the wipers do not move slowly enough to match the aggravatingly slow rate of accumulation on the windshield. Soon, the wipers begin to bounce and squeak. In frustration, you reach for the windshield wiper switch and turn it on and off, to suit your needs. This maneuver seems to do the job, but it also takes your attention away from the road and manages to keep one hand continuously occupied. In general, it makes for unsafe and unpleasant driving.

With the windshield-wiper electronic controller shown in Fig. 5-1, you can have complete speed control over your car's windshield wipers. They can be slowed down to any rate that suits your needs—even down to four sweeps per minute.

## HOW IT WORKS

The windshield-wiper controller has two principal circuits: the rate-determining circuit and the actuator (Fig. 5-2). The rate-determining circuit consists of a unijunction transistor connected as a free-running oscillator. The rate of the pulse

**Fig. 5-1. Windshield-wiper controller.**

output at base 1 (B1) of the unijunction transistor (Q1) is determined by the combination of C1 and the sum of R1 and R2. When the voltage across C1 reaches a predetermined value, Q1 suddenly conducts and C1 discharges through R4, producing a positive pulse. This pulse is applied to the gate (G) of the silicon-controlled rectifier which is the actuator. Placed in series with the +12-volt feed to the wiper motor, the SCR "latches" when triggered, turning on the wiper motor. At the end of each operating cycle, the return (parking) switch in

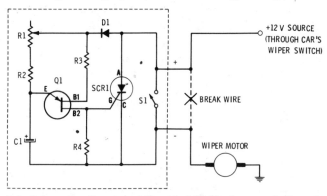

**Fig. 5-2. Schematic diagram of the windshield-wiper controller circuit.**

the wiper mechanism removes the dc voltage or reverses the motor connections, which turns off the SCR and brings the wiper blades to rest. However, as long as S1 is open, capacitor C1 will again begin to charge until the unijunction transistor conducts once more and the cycle repeats. Connection of the controller in no way affects the usual operation of the car's wiper switch. When the controller is turned off, switch S1 closes and shunts the SCR, bypassing the controller circuit for normal operation of the windshield wiper.

Operation of the controller can easily be checked with a 12-volt bulb. Place the bulb in series with one of the leads and connect the controller to a 12-volt source, observing t e correct polarity. The bulb will turn on after a delay determined by the setting of R1. To turn it off and check for the next cycle, the voltage source must be momentarily removed.

CAUTION: Do not connect the controller directly across a 12-volt source, since this will immediately burn out the SCR. A load must be connected in series with the controller and the power source.

## CONSTRUCTION

The controller is housed in a 3¼-inch × 2⅛-inch × 1⅝-inch aluminum minibox, and all of the circuit components are mounted on a 1¾-inch × 2¾-inch perf board, which is held in place by an extra nut on the control. A cardboard "antishort" shim is used to prevent any possibility of the components' shorting to the aluminum case. The SCR is mounted on a small L-shaped metal bracket. (The SCR is a heavy-duty type, and its operating cycle is short enough to make the use of a heatsink unnecessary.) The parts layout is shown in Fig. 5-3. The wire leads to the wiper switch should be at least No. 16 stranded wire and no longer than necessary, since a current of several amperes is being switched.

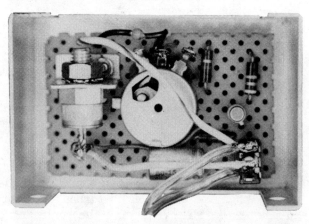

Fig. 5-3. Internal view of the windshield-wiper controller.

The controller can be mounted in any convenient location on the dash. It is held in place by means of screws through the surface of the U-shaped channel of the minibox.

### Table 5-1. Windshield-Wiper Controller Parts List

C1—50-$\mu$F, 15-V dc electrolytic capacitor
D1—silicon diode, type 1N5060 or equiv
Q1—2N2646 Unijunction transistor or equiv.

R1—1-megohm potentiometer, linear taper (Mallory U54 or equiv)
R2—22,000-ohm, ½-W resistor
R3, R4—220-ohm, ½-W resistor
S1—miniature spst toggle
SCR1—siilcon-controlled rectifier (G.E. type GEMR-4 or equiv)
Misc—3¼″ × 2⅛″ × 1⅝″ aluminum minibox (Bud CU-2101A or equiv); 1¾″ × 2¾″ perf board; sleeving for diode D1; heavy utility wire for hookup to wiper switch; extra nut for R1 shaft; 1¾″ × 2¾″ cardboard antishort shim; angle bracket for SCR1.

# 6

# AC OUTLET FOR
# YOUR CAR OR CAMPER

Ever wish you had a "live" 115-volt wall outlet on a camping trip? With the portable transistorized inverter shown in Fig. 6-1, you can have one. It gives you approximately 115-volts ac from a 12-volt car or camper battery so you can have a 115-volt wall outlet right on your dashboard. While the power capacity is limited to 100 watts, this is enough to run many small electrical conveniences you normally enjoy only at home, such as a stereo phonograph, radio receiver, tape recorder, electric shaver, lamps up to 100 watts, or even a small tv set.

The parts all fit in a 6-inch × 5-inch × 4-inch aluminum minibox with a carrying handle on top. This unit is small enough to store easily in a glove compartment. A flush-type receptacle is mounted on one end along with a pilot light and the on/off switch. You can plug directly into this outlet or use an extension cord if you want power at some other remote location, such as on a tailgate in a station wagon or inside a tent near the car.

The inverter is designed for use with 12-volt, negative-ground systems, which are the most common type used today. It is very important to observe correct polarity so that the power transistors will not be damaged. For quick, easy hookup, the input leads can be wired to a handy cigarette-lighter accessory plug available at auto-supply stores. The plug can then be inserted in the cigarette-lighter socket on the dashboard whenever you want ac power. When not in use, the inverter can be unplugged and stored away. For maximum efficiency, however, it is best to connect the positive lead of the inverter directly to the positive battery terminal, and the negative lead to a ground connection on the car.

In either case, use heavy, 12-gauge stranded wire since the inverter leads must be capable of handling a hefty current flow. If the wires are thin or the connections weak, the ac output will be reduced.

**Fig. 6-1. Portable ac outlet.**

At the heart of the inverter is a Triad TY-75A step-up transformer. As shown in Fig. 6-2, the center tap of the transformer primary (black lead) goes to the positive terminal of the 12-volt supply. The two halves of the primary winding are connected to identical transistor circuits. The transistors conduct alternately, producing a current flow first in one half of the primary winding, then in the other half. This, in turn, creates a stepped-up alternating current in the secondary winding. Since the transistors turn on and off 60 times a second, the current in the secondary winding has a frequency of 60 cycles to match that of regular house current. The transistors should be high-power germanium pnp types, such as the ones specified in the parts list. If you consider other types, be sure they have

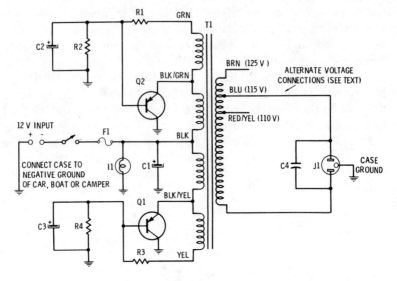

Fig. 6-2. Schematic of the inverter circuit.

the following minimum specifications: breakdown voltage of 36 volts, beta of 50, and power rating of 150 watts.

## HOW IT WORKS

When switch S1 is closed, a current step is applied to the bases of both transistors Q1 and Q2 through the center-tap connection of T1 and biasing resistors R1, R2, R3, and R4. Either Q1 or Q2 will turn on faster than its mate (it does not matter which). As one transistor reaches saturation, current flow through that half of T1 connected to the emitter of the saturated transistor becomes steady. Energy stored in the field surrounding that half of the transformer primary winding is instantly restored to the circuit as the flux collapses back through T1. This induces a large pulse in the primary winding which is applied to both transistor bases. The pulse polarity drives the transistor that is on toward off, and it drives the transistor that is off toward on. When saturation is reached in the second transistor, the cycle repeats. Capacitors C1, C2, C3, and C4 filter out transients that might adversely affect the circuit operation. The output power is taken from the tapped secondary of transformer T1. In the event of a short on the secondary circuit, energy needed to sustain oscillation is drained from the primary circuit without damaging the transistors. Fuse F1 protects the primary circuit.

As shown in Fig. 6-3, the transformer is bolted to the end of the minibox but is placed on the bottom to carry its weight. The transistors are mounted on the outside at the back (Fig. 6-4) for good ventilation and cooling. Because these transistors handle large currents and get warm, it is also important to fasten them firmly to the minibox so that it acts as a good heat sink. When connecting the transistors, note the markings on the leads to determine which is the base and which is the emitter. Most large power transistors of the type used here are stamped with a "B" and "E" to indicate the base and emitter. The metal case itself serves as the collector. If the transistor is not marked, hold it so that the two leads are horizontal and slightly above the centerline of the case. The lead on the left is the base, and the lead on the right the emitter.

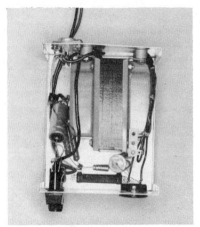
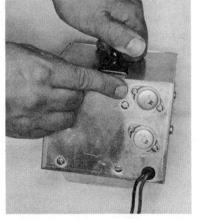

Fig. 6-3. Internal view of the inverter.    Fig. 6-4. Location of power transistors on back of inverter.

You will find there are three output taps on the transformer, which offers you a choice of voltages. It is necessary to select the tap that gives the closest to the desired voltage. Start with the blue lead and check the output voltage with a voltmeter. If the voltage is low, disconnect the blue lead and try the brown one. If the voltage is high, use the red/yellow lead. If a voltmeter is not available, compare the intensity of a 100-watt light bulb first on regular house current, then on the inverter. The bulb should have about the same brightness on either source. It it seems too dim, connect the higher-voltage tap; if too bright, connect the lower-voltage tap. As shown in Fig. 6-3, use lug-type terminal strips for making connections between components. Do not operate the inverter without a load plugged into the outlet.

## Table 6-1. Portable AC Outlet Parts List

C1—250-$\mu$F, 25-V dc electrolytic capacitor
C2, C3—2-$\mu$F, 50-V dc electrolytic capacitor
C4—1-$\mu$F, 400-V dc capacitor
R1, R3—5.1-ohm, 5-W resistor
R2, R4—200-ohm, 20-W resistor
T1—step-up transformer (Triad TY-75A or equiv)
I1—12-V indicator lamp assembly (Industrial Devices B3060D1, or equiv)
J1—single ac receptacle
Q1, Q2—high-power germanium pnp transistor (Motorola HEP G6009 or equiv); alternative transistors: 2N3637, 2N3638, or 2N3639
S1—heavy-duty spst toggle switch, 10-A minimum rating
F1—10-A 3AG fuse and fuseholder (Littelfuse 342001A or equiv)
Case—6″ × 5″ × 4″ aluminum minibox (Bud CU-2107A or equiv)

# 7

# OIL-LEVEL CHECKER

Very few motorists are aware of the fact that accurate oil-level readings are only possible after the engine has stopped for at least two hours, giving the oil a chance to drip back into the pan. The "idiot" light or the oil gauge in your car reads oil *pressure*, but you must still make sure that you have enough oil to maintain proper lubrication.

With the electronic oil-level checker shown in Fig. 7-1, you can now be sure of proper oil level before you begin the day's driving. All you have to do before you start your engine is to press the TEST button on the programmed oil-level checker, and logic circuits will read a remote sensor and tell you if the oil level is all right or if you need to add a quart. This is all done from *within* the car, without lifting the hood, or pulling the dipstick.

## HOW IT WORKS

The transistors and diodes combine to make up the *timing circuit*, the *voltage-sensitive switch* and the *logic circuit*, as shown in Fig. 7-2. The timing circuit controls the power applied to a small glass-encased thermistor that is attached to the car's dipstick, opposite the "add one quart" mark. This circuit assures that power is applied long enough to try to heat the thermistor, thereby attempting to change its resistance. Transistor Q1 and Q2 form a monostable multivibrator with cir-

**Fig. 7-1. Oil-level checker.**

cuit values selected to give a time constant of about 25 seconds.

The schematic diagram for the oil-level checker circuit is shown in Fig. 7-3. When power switch S1 is in the ON position, transistor Q3 is on and no voltage is available across thermistor T, since the circuit is shunted by Q3. This is the normal state of the circuit when power is applied. When the TEST switch is depressed, the base of transistor Q1 is pulsed with a positive voltage, which causes its collector voltage to drop to zero volts and charge the two parallel-connected 200-$\mu$F capacitors (C2 and C3). Transistor Q2, which is normally on, is turned off by the charge on the capacitors, and its collector voltage rises to 12 volts. Resistor R5, connected from the collector of Q2 to the base of Q1, feeds back sustaining voltage to maintain the monostable condition for a period of 25 seconds, as determined by the time constant of C2, C3, and R3.

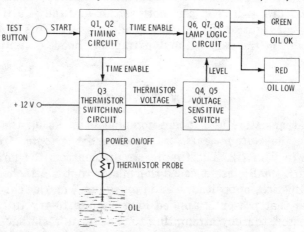

**Fig. 7-2. Functional diagram of the oil-level checker.**

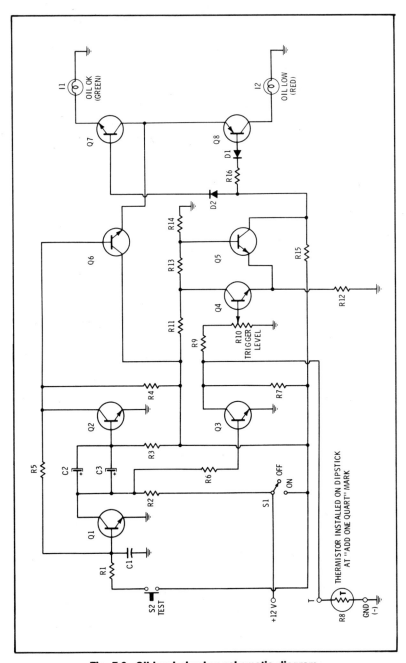

**Fig. 7-3. Oil-level checker schematic diagram.**

51

While the timing circuit is in operation, transistor Q3 is turned off and 12 volts is applied to the thermistor through resistor R7. Current flows through the thermistor for a period of 25 seconds.

The characteristics of the thermistor are such that, with current flowing through the device, its resistance will decrease as a result of the increase in its absolute temperature. The temperature of the thermistor is a function of the physical area of the thermistor. Thus, if we increase the effective thermal radiation area of the thermistor by placing it in contact with the cold oil in the crankcase, we have essentially a huge "heat sink" capable of absorbing the heat of the thermistor. The heat sink prevents the thermistor from heating itself up and decreasing its resistance. However, if the thermistor is not in contact with oil, its temperature will increase rapidly due to the current flowing through it and, hence, its resistance will decrease sharply.

A voltage divider consisting of R9 and R10 is connected across the thermistor, and whatever voltage appears across the thermistor will also appear across the voltage divider. Potentiometer R10 permits a trigger level to be set for the Schmitt trigger consisting of Q4 and Q5. This circuit is used to detect the voltage level across the thermistor (which corresponds to its resistance), thereby detecting whether the thermistor is in contact with oil or is in free air. With the power switch ON and the TEST switch depressed, transistor Q4 senses the relatively high voltage level present across the thermistor, which has not yet begun to heat. As a result, Q4 becomes conductive. This turns off transistor Q5, and a positive voltage is available at its collector, which is coupled through diode D2 to the base of Q7. Transistor Q6 and Q7 connected in series form an AND circuit. Transistor Q6 receives an enabling input from the collector of Q2, which becomes positive when the TEST switch is depressed. The green lamp lights up, since both Q6 and Q7 are conductive.

So long as the thermistor resistance does not decrease, the voltage level available across R9 and R10 remains steady and the green lamp will remain on. This condition can occur only when the thermistor is in contact with cold oil. If the thermistor is not in contact with the oil, its resistance will decrease as it heats itself up within the timing period, and the voltage at the base of Q4 will fall below the trigger level of the Schmitt trigger. Transistor Q4 will turn off and transistor Q5 will turn on, causing the voltage at its collector to essentially fall to zero volts and thus removing the enabling input to transistor Q7. The green lamp then turns off because Q7 is no longer conductive. Simultaneously, when transistor Q5 becomes conductive, it turns on transistor Q8, which, with Q6, forms a complementary AND circuit. With transistor Q6 still enabled by a positive input from Q2, and Q8 now becoming conductive, the red lamp will illuminate, indicating that the oil is low.

The green lamp and red lamp can *never* be on *simultaneously*. The logic of the circuit is such that *either* the green lamp *or* the red lamp *must* be on, but never *both*. Let us now discuss the significance of the circuit.

Power switch S1 is arranged so that it primarily controls power to the major circuits. However, the 12-volt supply is always connected to the collector of Q1 through resistor R2. Thus, an accumulated charge is maintained on capacitors C2 and C3 to ensure continuous timing accuracy and prevent false triggering during the period of time when the unit is first turned on.

## CALIBRATION

With the thermistor in free air, connect a dc voltmeter across its terminals. Turn the switch off and connect the oil-level checker to the positive and negative terminals of the 12-volt supply. Let the unit sit for two minutes to accumulate the initial charge on capacitors C2 and C3 to prevent false triggering. Depress the TEST switch and observe the thermistor voltage on the voltmeter. The voltage reading decreases from its initial reading of about 6 volts to about 2 or 3 volts as the thermistor heats up. Let the unit cycle out, disregarding any indications of the lamps, and let the thermistor cool off for one minute. Then push the TEST button again and observe that the voltmeter reading decays after the button is released. As the voltage crosses the 3-volt level, adjust the potentiometer so that the green lamp, which should have been on, goes off and the red lamp turns on. This sets the switching level of the Schmitt trigger so that it flips back to the so-called normal conditions when the voltage decays to about one-half of what it was when power was actually applied to the thermistor. This is because after about 6 seconds of operation in free air, the thermistor resistance should have dropped from its initial value of 1000 ohms to about 500 ohms. Again, let the unit cycle out, wait one minute for the thermistor to cool, and depress the TEST button again. Note that the green lamp comes on and remains on for a couple of seconds. As the thermistor reheats and its resistance decreases, the voltage level drops to 3 volts, the green lamp goes off, and the red lamp comes on. The red lamp remains on until the timing cycle of 25 seconds is over, at which time the red lamp goes off. Wait one minute and then hold the thermistor between your fingers or immerse it in a glass of water. Again depress the TEST button. Note that the green lamp stays on as long as you provide additional heat-sinking action.

**Fig. 7-4. Internal view of the oil-level checker.**

## ASSEMBLY

The unit is built on perf board, and the component layout is easily followed from the photographs. The lamps, switches, and terminal board are mounted on one-half of a minibox, as shown in Fig. 7-4. The circuit board is fastened by four 1-inch screws which go through $\frac{5}{16}$-inch spacers to maintain proper spacing between the board and the minibox to prevent shorts. The oil dipstick in your car is modified by adding the thermistor so that the "bead" is just at the "add 1 quart" mark (see Fig. 7-5). The thermistor support is a small piece of dowel rod,

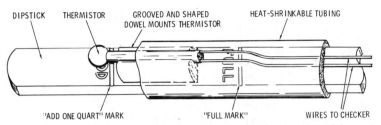

**Fig. 7-5. Modified oil dipstick showing placement of the thermistor.**

shaped to be slightly narrower than the dipstick and grooved to keep the thermistor centered and away from the dipstick itself. The bead should also be about ¼-inch away from the support.

Carefully solder two insulated wires to the thermistor leads and slip short pieces of heat-shrinkable tubing over them. The thermistor and its support are held onto the dipstick with the heat-shrinkable tubing which is then shrunk by putting the whole assembly in an oven preheated to about 200°F. It may also be wise to reduce the width of the dipstick slightly along the length of the heat-shrinkable tubing to be sure that the width does not exceed the inside diameter of the dipstick hole.

### USING THE OIL-LEVEL CHECKER

Connect the instrument's (+) and (−) terminals to a fused 12-volt line that does not go through the ignition switch, and connect the wires from the dipstick to the (T) and (−) terminals. Insert the dipstick to the usual depth.

Press the TEST button. Depending on your oil level, the green lamp will go on and stay on, or the red lamp will come on.

NOTE: The checker is meant to be used *before* start-up, while the oil level is at its highest and while the oil is at ambient temperature. Obviously, oil temperature will be high in a running engine, and this will prevent "self-heat" of the thermistor from being detectable, since ambient temperature is already high. (*No* device can measure oil level accurately in a running engine because the oil is not all in the reservoir pan but is circulating throughout the engine, where it should be!)

## Table 7-1. Oil-Level Checker Parts List

C1—.1-$\mu$F, 100-V dc capacitor

C2, C3—200-$\mu$F, 15-V dc electrolytic capacitor

D1, D2—1-A, 50-V silicon diode, type 1N5060 or equiv

I1—12-V red indicator lamp (Industrial Devices B3060D1 or equiv)

I2—12-V green indicator lamp (Industrial Devices B3060D5 or equiv)

Q1, Q2, Q3—npn silicon transistor, type 2N3414 or equiv

Q4, Q5—npn silicon transistor, type 2N5172 or equiv

Q6, Q7—npn silicon transistor, type D42C5 or equiv

Q8—pnp silicon transistor, type D43C5 or equiv

R1, R6—10,000-ohm, ½-W ±10% resistor

R2, R4, R7—1000-ohm, ½-W ±10% resistor

R3—62,000-ohm, ½-W ±10% resistor

R5—22,000-ohm, ½-W ±10% resistor

R8—glass probe thermistor, 1K at 25°C (Fenwal Electronics GB31M2— DO NOT SUBSTITUTE)

R9, R13, R15, R16—2700-ohm, ½-W ±10% resistor

R10—5000-ohm potentiometer (Mallory MTC53L4 or equiv)

R11—4700-ohm, ½-W ±10% resistor

R12—68-ohm, ½-W ±10% resistor

R14—6800-ohm, ½-W ±10% resistor

S1—spst subminiature toggle switch

S2—normally open push-button switch

Misc—5¼″ × 3″ × 2⅛″ aluminum minibox (Bud CU-2106A or equiv), 4⅛″ × 2⅜″ perf board, hardware, wire, solder, etc.

# 8

# REMINDERLIGHT

The road ahead is narrow and dark. As your car plunges into the gloom, its headlights splash twin pathways of illumination across the blacktop pavements. Beyond, the road, landscape, and sky merge in an inky, monochromatic blackness. Suddenly, a huge, jagged pothole flashes briefly into view. You swerve. *Too late!* The left front wheel drops. *Slam!* It strikes the opposite edge of the hole and rebounds upward, returning to the pavement with a hollow thud! You regain control, but your visibility now seems limited—one of the headlamps is not working. You flick the dimmer switch, but the low beams do not respond on that side either.

Is this condition serious? Safety experts say: *"Yes!"* Your car's sealed-beam headlamps are designed to provide good road illumination. But, they also serve as visual "marker beacons" to the driver of an oncoming vehicle. Headlamp spacing and their height above ground help the approaching driver identify your vehicle as an automobile. The changing distance between the approaching two beams gives a fair measure of how far away your vehicle is and helps him to approximate the closing speed. Most important, however, your car's headlamps give the other driver an idea of the width of your car and where it is on the road with respect to his own vehicle. Take away *one* headlamp and all of these visual clues are lost to the approaching driver. Your car becomes a "one-eyed menace."

Detroit has put some changes into effect on late-model cars, however, that promise to eliminate this hazard. Through some special wiring provisions, carmakers have tied the parking lamps to the headlamp circuit so that both sets of lamps glow when the headlamps are turned on. If a headlamp fails, the parking lamps remain operative so that the oncoming driver still receives the visual clues he needs to pass by safely.

Both the authors own vintage cars, neither of which has this desirable feature. We decided to add the feature to our cars, and while we were about it, a second idea presented itself. Like many other forgetful drivers who park and lock their cars and walk away oblivious to the headlights they have left blazing, both of us have suffered bruised egos and the inconvenience of dead batteries as a result of our forgetfulness. So, we have combined a parking-lights-on-with-headlights safety feature and an indicator to show that the headlights are on when the ignition is off. The result is the "Reminderlight" (Fig. 8-1).

Featuring just three major components—two silicon diodes and a self-flashing lamp—the Reminderlight assembles in only a few minutes. The two silicon diodes are soldered to the lamp and mounted inside a plastic pill container (usually available

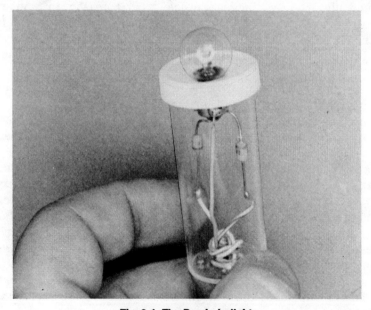

**Fig. 8-1. The Reminderlight.**

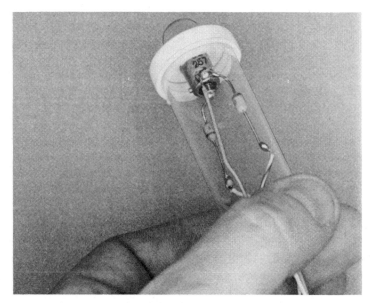

**Fig. 8-2. Internal connections for the Reminderlight.**

for the asking at any drugstore). The self-flashing lamp mounts in the soft plastic cap of the container, and the leads are soldered to the free end of the diodes and the shell of the lamps, as shown in Fig. 8-2. Ordinary 20-gauge hookup wire can be used for the leads. Refer to the schematic in Fig. 8-3 for the correct diode polarity.

An exit hole in the bottom end of the container permits the leads to be passed to the outside, where they are attached to the car's wiring. The diodes and leads are simply inserted into the snug-fitting container, and the plastic cap bearing the bulb is snapped into place, affording a neat, easy-to-install assembly.

## HOW IT WORKS

The schematic of the Reminderlight is given in Fig. 8-3. Only three leads need be connected to the car wiring. Lead 1 connects the anode of diode D1 to the headlamp circuit, and lead 2 attaches to the parking-lamp circuit. Lead 3 connects to the wire that runs from the oil-pressure sensing switch (usually located on the side of the engine block) to the instrument panel OIL indicator. In most cars, you can make all the required connections without going under the hood, since all affected circuits are usually accessible under the dash. Because diode D1 allows current to flow in only one direction, current cannot flow through D1 to the headlamps when the parking lamps are on. But, when the headlamp circuit is energized, D1 conducts so that power is also applied to the parking-lamp circuit. This simple arrangement yields the parking-lamp safety feature found in all late-model cars.

The reminder portion of the circuit comprises lamp I1 and diode D2. Lamp I1 is a special flasher lamp (available from the source specified in the parts list). This lamp has a built-in bimetallic element which is in series with the lamp filament. When the filament is energized, it imparts heat to the bimetallic element causing it to bend. At it bends backward, it breaks the circuit to the filament and the lamp extinguishes. The bimetallic element cools and restores the power to the filament, and another cycle commences. The result is an attention-getting flashing action, bright enough to be seen in daylight.

To make the circuit operative, +12 volts must be present at the cathode of diode D1 (either from the headlamp or from the parking-lamp circuit), and a ground must be present on

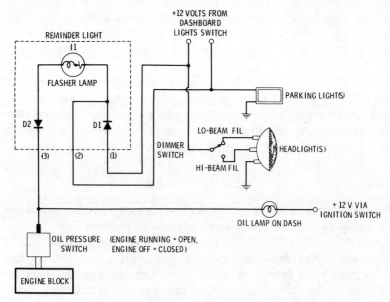

Fig. 8-3. Reminderlight schematic and external connections.

the cathode of diode D2. The oil-pressure sensor switch provides the necessary logic. When the engine is operating, oil pressure forces the contacts of this switch apart, breaking the circuit to ground. (That is why your OIL indicator stays off as long as oil pressure is normal.) But, when the engine is off, the sensor contacts close, effectively grounding the cathode of D2. This forms a ground path for current to flow through lamp I1, *if* you have shut off the engine but left the lights on. Of course, turning off the lights will remove power from the lamp.

## INSTALLATION

The Reminderlight may be installed at any convenient point under the dash or on the steering column. You can fashion a strap or bracket to hold it in place or use plastic electrical tape to bind it to a convenient supporting member. Wire 1 may be connected to the lead that runs from the headlight switch to the floor-mounted dimmer switch. Connect it to the lead that goes to the movable switch arm so that the parking lights will be on, regardless of the dimmer switch position (high- or low-beam). Connect lead 2 to the wire that goes to the parking-lamp circuit. Lead 3 connects to the wire from your engine's oil-pressure sensor switch. In all cases, carefully skin the existing wire with a razor blade to expose the conductor. Then, wrap the lead from the Reminderlight tightly around the exposed conductor and insulate the connection with good-quality plastic electrical tape. Your best guide to wiring identification is the manufacturer's shop manual. If you do not have one, check with your local dealer's service department for the correct wire colors and hookup information.

Once you have put the Reminderlight into service, you will never have to pay any further attention to it. That is, not until it flashes a warning to save your battery by shutting off your lights, or until it averts a tragedy on the highway by keeping your car from becoming a "one-eyed menace."

### Table 8-1. Reminderlight Parts List

D1, D2—2-A, 50-piv silicon diode (RCA SK3081 or equiv)
I1—No. 257 self-flashing lamp
Misc—1″ dia × 2″ long plastic pill container, wire, solder

# 9

# VOLTMINDER FOR YOUR CAR

This easy-to-build instrument analyzes the condition of all automotive electrical circuits. It checks ground connections and voltage levels at the starter motor, starter switch, voltage regulator, generator or alternator, all lights, distributor, ignition primary circuit, and fuses.

The Voltminder shown in Fig. 9-1 is easily constructed. It is housed in a 3¾-inch × 6-inch × 2-inch plastic utility case whose metal cover is cut to fit a standard meter. The range-selector switch and binding posts are also conveniently located on the front panel.

A schematic and pictorial layout of the Voltminder are shown in Fig. 9-2. The NORMAL range of this instrument measures direct (dc) voltages from 0 to 18 volts. The EXPANDED range covers 11 through 16 volts over the full length of the scale. This yields a 3 to 1 scale-expansion factor, which permits precise observation of voltage levels within the selected range. Each voltage range is individually calibrated by means of miniature resistance trimmer controls. These controls (R3 and R4) are mounted, together with two fixed resistors and a diode, on a small perf board that is secured directly to the meter terminals. The trimmer controls are supported by their terminals, which are soldered directly to the leads on the other side of the perf board. Flea clips are used as tie points. Fig. 9-2B clearly shows the internal layout. Be sure that both binding posts are insulated from the metal front panel to prevent shorts. The Voltminder can be used either with test prods for servicing and troubleshooting or with an adapter that fits directly into the cigarette lighter for continuous monitoring of the battery voltage.

Fig. 9-1. The Voltminder.

The indicating meter is a standard 0 to 1 milliampere movement with the scale calibration changed in order to adapt it for the Voltminder. A full-size new scale appears in Fig. 9-3. You can have a photostat made at any local print shop, or you can trace this illustration directly.

In order to achieve the expanded-scale characteristic, a zener diode is used. This semiconductor component has the ability to regulate voltage within precise limits. In this case we are using a 10-volt zener diode, which does not "break down" until at least 10 volts is applied. The zener diode prevents the meter from showing any indication at all until at least a 10-volt potential appears across the meter leads. Then, the diode allows current to pass and the meter begins to indicate. Thus, with the switch set to the EXPANDED range, there will be no meter indication until more than 10-volts dc is applied to the Voltminder input terminals.

## CALIBRATION

It takes just a few minutes to calibrate both ranges of the Voltminder. This is done by adjusting the trimmer resistors (R3, R4, and R5) so that voltage readings correspond with those of another calibrated "standard" voltmeter.

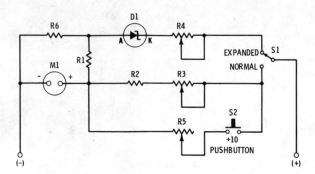

(A) Schematic.

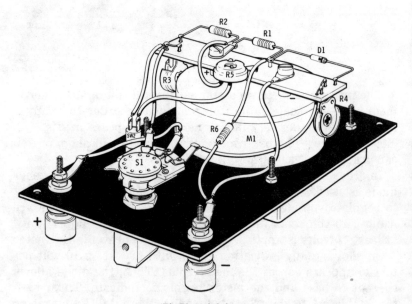

(B) Pictorial layout.

**Fig. 9-2. Schematic and pictorial layout of the Voltminder.**

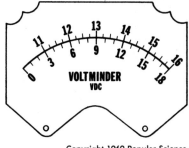

**Fig. 9-3. Full-size calibrated scale for the Voltminder.**

Set the range switch to NORMAL and apply a known dc voltage to the (+) and (−) terminals. This voltage could be from a car battery or from any variable low-voltage dc supply. Check the reading of the standard voltmeter. Adjust trimmer control R3 with a small screwdriver until the Voltmeter indicates the same voltage as the standard voltmeter. Now switch to the EXPANDED range and similarly adjust trimmer R4. Switch the Voltminder back and forth between the EXPANDED and NORMAL ranges. If the instrument is correctly calibrated, the readings will be identical for all voltages between 11 and 16 volts on both scales. Calibrate the ÷10 scale with the known voltage of a single flashlight battery. Connect the battery to the (+) and (−) terminals of both meters and adjust R5 until the standard meter and the Voltminder indicate the battery voltage (nominally 1.4 volts, which gives a reading of 14 on the Voltminder).

## WHAT CIRCUITS DOES THE VOLTMINDER CHECK?

Corresponding numbers in the typical electrical system of Fig. 9-4 show how the Voltminder tests every aspect of a 12-volt system. Since most of the tests check several components, there is considerable overlap, but this is ideal for isolating a problem. If you get a poor meter reading in all tests involving a given component, you know exactly where your trouble lies.

## HOW TO USE THE VOLTMINDER

### Cranking Voltage Test

This test quickly determines whether or not sufficient voltage is being delivered to the ignition system while the engine is

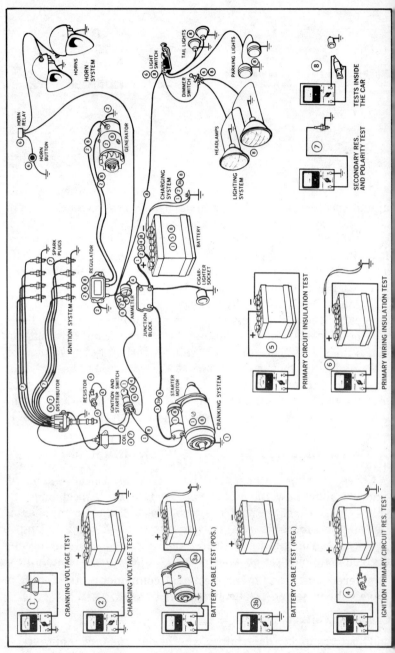

Fig. 9-4. Electrical hookup and tests using the Voltminder.

cranking. A normal reading confirms that the general condition of the battery, cables, starting system, and the circuit to the ignition system is satisfactory. An unsatisfactory reading may indicate that further testing or examination is required in this area. To perform the test:

1. Connect the (+) and (−) leads of the Voltminder to the ignition-coil primary and ground, as shown in Fig. 9-4.
2. Set the Voltminder switch to NORMAL range.
3. Short the primary winding of the ignition coil with a clip-lead jumper or remove the lead from the ignition-coil tower so that the engine cannot start.
4. With the ignition switch ON, crank the engine for five seconds and observe the Voltminder reading. The cranking voltage should not be less than 9.5 volts.

*Results and Indications*

Meter reads specified voltage or more; cranking speed normal and even—battery, starter, cables, switch, and ignition circuit to coil operating satisfactorily.

Meter reads less than specified voltage—weak battery, defective cables, poor connections, defective switch or starter, or defective ignition circuit to coil. (Check for defective ballast-resistor bypass in primary circuit of ignition coil.)

Cranking speed is below normal—excessive resistance in cables or starting motor. Excessive mechanical drag in engine (check oil grade).

Cranking speed is irregular—uneven compression, or defective starter or starter drive.

## Charging Voltage Test

The charging voltage test provides a good overall indication of the voltage available to the entire electrical system. The voltage applied to the ignition system is an important factor to be considered when cases of distributor-point burning are encountered and when other electrical components are found to have subnormal operating lives.

In cases where subnormal charging-voltage readings are encountered, it is suggested that each component in the charging system be tested to determine exactly where the malfunction lies within the system.

1. Set the Voltminder switch to the EXPANDED position.
2. Observing the correct polarity, connect the (+) and (−) leads to the insulated post of the battery and to ground, as shown in Fig. 9-4, or to the battery terminal of the voltage regulator and to ground, depending on which is more accessible.
3. Operate the engine at a speed of 1500 to 2000 rpm.
4. Note the Voltminder reading after meter pointer stops climbing. The meter reading should be between 13.5 and 15.0 volts.

*Results and Indications*

Charging voltage is within the specified charging-voltage range for the vehicle being tested—charging system and voltage regulator operating satisfactorily.

Charging voltage is below specified range—defective generator (alternator) or drive system, defective or maladjusted voltage regulator, high resistance in charging circuit.

Charging voltage is above specified voltage range—defective or maladjusted voltage regulator, high resistance in regulator ground circuit, or defective field circuit.

## Battery Cable Tests

Defective or undersize battery cables, loose or corroded connections, or excessively long cables can easily be the cause of inefficient starting-system operation, improper charging-system operation, or malfunction in many parts of the vehicle's electrical system. Defective cables and/or connections result in excessive voltage drop during operation of the starting motor. The battery should be fully charged, and the starter current draw must be within normal limits when battery cable tests are conducted. (If any doubt exists concerning the condition of the battery or the starting motor, these components should be tested by your local mechanic with a battery/starter tester.)

*Positive Battery Cable Test*

The entire insulated portion of a cranking circuit may be tested in one operation, or each individual portion of the insulated circuit may be tested separately to pinpoint an indicated defect.

1. Set the Voltminder switch to the NORMAL position. Remove the lead from the ignition-coil tower to prevent the engine from starting.
2. Connect the (+) lead from the Voltminder to the center of the positive battery post and the (−) lead to the input terminal of the starting motor, as shown in Fig. 9-4 (3a), observing proper polarity. (Meter will attempt to indicate battery voltage until the ignition switch is closed.)
3. Operate starting motor and observe the Voltminder reading. Generally, the meter reading should not exceed 0.5 volt on most vehicles.

*Negative (Ground) Battery Cable Test*

1. Set the Voltminder switch to the NORMAL position.
2. Connect (+) lead from the Voltminder to a ground on the engine block and the (−) lead to the center of the negative post of the battery as shown in Fig. 9-4 (3b). Repeat Step 3 of the previous test.

*Results and Indications*

Meter readings are within specified limits—cables, connections, etc., in normal operating condition.

Meter readings exceed specified limits—defective cable, undersized cable, loose or corroded connections, defective starter solenoid contacts, starter motor drawing excessive current, etc.

When above-normal voltage-drop readings are obtained, retest each item and connection within that portion of the circuit to determine the exact location of the fault. Correct the fault by cleaning and tightening connections or by replacing cables or components, as necessary, and then retest.

## Ignition Primary-Circuit Resistance Test*

An excessive voltage drop in the ignition primary circuit between the battery and the ignition coil can reduce the secondary output of the ignition coil to the extent that hard starting and poor performance can result. This test checks the low-voltage ignition (primary circuit) wiring, including the ballast resistor (if used).

---

* Where the vehicle is equipped with a solid-state ignition system, special checks may be required.

NOTE: On some vehicles, a special type of resistance wire is built into the wiring harness to serve the same purpose as a separate ballast-resistor unit.

1. Turn the Voltminder selector switch to the NORMAL position.
2. Connect the Voltminder leads as follows (observe proper polarity) : from battery (+) terminal to the high side of the ballast resistor, for coils equipped with an external ballast resistor, as shown in Fig. 9-4 (4). (From battery (+) terminal to the high side of the coil primary, for coils not equipped with an external ballast resistor.)
3. Use a jumper lead to ground the primary terminal of the distributor (lead from low end of coil primary). Grounding the distributor primary terminal with the jumper lead makes it unnecessary to spot the engine so that the breaker points are closed, and also eliminates the possibility of false test readings due to reduced current caused by defective points, wiring, and connections in the distributor.
4. Be sure all lights and accessories are turned off.
5. Turn the ignition switch on (do not crank engine) and observe the meter. The Voltminder should not read more than 0.5 volt.
6. Test the ignition switch by turning it off and on several times. The Voltminder should read the same each time the switch is turned on.
7. Test all ignition primary wires for tightness. Move them about and note any change in the meter reading with the ignition switch on.

*Results and Indications*

Meter is indicating within specified limits—connections, wiring, switch contacts, etc., in satisfactory condition.

Meter readings exceed the specified maximum—loose or corroded connections, undersized or faulty wiring, damaged or worn ignition switch contacts, etc.

If the meter readings exceed the specified maximum, isolate the point of high resistance by placing the test leads across each connection and wire, in turn. The reading across a connection should be zero. The reading across any one wire should be proportionate to its length, as compared to the length and allowable voltage drop of the engine circuit.

## Primary Circuit (12-Volt System) Insulation Tests

Defective insulation in the primary circuit or at the battery can result in a constant loss of energy from the battery. Trouble of this nature is usually indicated by the fact that the battery becomes discharged if the weather is damp or if the vehicle has not been used for a day or two. Usually, leakage of this nature is so gradual that it is impossible to detect it on the charge indicator of the vehicle (if one is provided). These tests will reveal any major problem areas.

Electrolyte, dirt, moisture, or foreign material on the surface of the battery usually results in a continual battery discharge because this foreign material provides an electrical path between the battery terminals. Twelve-volt batteries are more susceptible to energy losses of this nature than six-volt batteries because of the higher voltage involved. It is always wise to keep the top of the battery as clean as possible to prevent formation of a leakage path. To check for leakage, proceed as follows:

1. Set the Voltminder switch to the NORMAL position.
2. Connect the negative (−) lead from the Voltminder to the negative post of the vehicle's battery, as shown in Fig. 9-4 (5).
3. Move the positive (+) lead around the top surfaces of the battery, being careful not to touch the positive battery post.
4. Observe the meter for indications

Any meter deflection indicates an energy loss due to dirt, moisture, or electrolyte on the external surfaces of the battery. When this condition exists, it is recommended that the battery be removed from the vehicle, thoroughly cleaned with a solution of baking soda or ammonia and water, and completely dried before reinstallation. It is also suggested that all dirt, moisture, corrosion, etc., be removed from the battery carrier. The cable connections should also be thoroughly cleaned. For dependable operation, make sure that the battery is in a state of full charge before reinstalling it in the vehicle.

## Primary-Wiring Insulation Test

This test of primary-wiring insulation can detect leakage in the insulation that is too small to be located with an ohmmeter test. Considering the many accessories operated from the 12-volt line, it is not unlikely that leakage may occur, in time, in one or more circuits.

1. Disconnect the ground (−) battery cable from the battery post. Connect the Voltminder leads as shown in Fig. 9-4 (6).
2. Turn off all switches and close all doors to prevent operation of the courtesy light from the door switches. Disconnect the underhood or trunk light (if used).
3. Turn the Voltminder switch to the NORMAL position.
4. If the vehicle is equipped with an electric clock, touch the battery cable to the battery post just prior to conducting the test, to rewind the clock, or leave the clock disconnected if your clock is the "continuous" type.
5. Note the Voltminder reading.

*Results and Indications*

Voltminder indicates zero—insulation in electrical primary circuits normal; no leakage exists.

Voltminder reads above zero—insulation leakage exists in one or more of the primary electrical circuits.

To locate leakage (an incomplete short) in the primary wiring circuits, remove the "hot" lead from each of the following components in the order in which they are listed. Retest the primary circuit for leaks after disconnecting each item.

| | |
|---|---|
| Stoplight switch | Accessory switches |
| Courtesy light switches | Domelight switch |
| Horn relay and wiring | Regulator |
| Ignition switch | Heater switch |
| Light switch | Capacitors (rfi suppression |
| Radio | and breaker-point bypass) |

NOTE: Capacitors may be located on the light switch, the regulator battery terminal, generator armature terminal, etc. Check your service manual for specific information.

## Secondary Resistance Check/Polarity Test

Excessive ignition-coil secondary circuit resistance uses up energy that is needed to maintain good ignition under all conditions. It also severely reduces ignition-system reserve and consequently results in poor performance under severe operating conditions. Incorrect secondary-system polarity can result in up to 40% more voltage being required to fire the spark plugs, causing misfire and erratic engine operation. Polarity error can be easily corrected by interchanging the two primary-circuit connections at the ignition coil. Test as follows:

1. To prevent the generator from operating during the test, disconnect the lead from the field terminal of the generator.

2. Start the engine and adjust the speed to 1500 rpm.
3. Set the Voltminder switch to NORMAL position. (Do not use the expanded scale.) *CAUTION: Beware of high voltage at spark plugs; use an insulated probe on the negative lead.*
4. Connect (+) lead to engine ground, and contact the (−) test lead to each spark-plug-wire terminal, in turn, as shown in Fig. 9-4 (7). *Do not remove hv cable from the spark plug.* The meter should deflect upscale, indicating low resistance and correct spark polarity. All readings should be the same.

*Results and Indications*

Readings are upscale and essentially equal—secondary circuit in normal condition.

All readings are very low—corroded coil tower terminal, poorly connected or broken coil wire, center distributor-cap electrode burned, burned rotor tip, open secondary in coil.

One or more readings are lower than average—broken or poorly connected spark-plug wires, burned or corroded distributor-cap terminals, gouged electrodes inside the distributor cap.

Readings are higher than average at two or more spark plugs—crossfire occurring in the distributor cap or between the spark-plug cables concerned.

Meter reads downscale—polarity error, reverse the primary-circuit connections at ignition coil.

## Battery Tests Inside the Car

With no current drain (all switches off), a good 12-volt battery should read between 12.2 and 12.8 volts, and a 6-volt battery should read between 6.1 and 6.4 volts. Voltages less than these indicate a weak battery.

It is normal for the battery voltage to drop somewhat under a heavy current drain—for example, when the starter motor is cranking the engine. The voltage of a good 12-volt battery may drop to about 9.5 volts, and a 6-volt battery may drop to about 4.75 volts under a 150- to 300-ampere starting load. A voltage drop of more than this indicates either a worn-out battery, poor cables or contacts, or a battery of insufficient capacity.

With the engine at a fast idle (about 1500 rpm) and all lights and accessories turned off, the charging voltage at the battery should be between 13.2 and 15.2 volts for a 12-volt battery and between 6.6 and 7.6 volts for a 6-volt battery.

Charging voltages lower than 6.6 volts in 6-volt systems or lower than 13.2 volts in 12-volt systems indicate either a faulty generator or alternator, a faulty or improperly adjusted voltage regulator, or a worn-out battery. Higher than specified voltages (generally 7.6 volts in 6-volt systems and 15.2 volts in 12-volt systems) indicate a faulty or improperly adjusted voltage regulator, poor battery-cable connections, or a defective battery. These values should be checked against the specifications for the electrical system being tested.

To make a Voltminder test of the battery from inside the car, proceed as follows:

1. Connect the cigarette-lighter adapter to the Voltminder leads (+ to tip; − to shell). Plug into the cigarette lighter to monitor the system voltage, as shown in Fig. 9-4 (8).
2. Check the battery condition from the front seat by observing the Voltminder (on the EXPANDED scale).
   a. Engine off; note voltage.
   b. Turn on lights; note voltage.
   c. Crank engine; note voltage.
   d. Engine running; note voltage.

Results:

    a. Engine-off voltage should be 12.0 volts.

    b. Lights-on voltage should be at least 11.8 volts (low beam).

    c. Cranking voltage should be 9.5 to 10.0 volts (at 70°F).

    d. Engine-running voltage should be at least 13.2 volts.

NOTE: The voltage readings given are for most makes and models of cars. Voltages may vary from car to car, based on battery age, condition, and temperature.

### Table 9-1. Voltminder Parts List

D1—10-V, ½-W zener diode (Sylvania ECG5019 or equiv)
R1—4700-ohm, ½-W ±10% resistor
R2—15,000-ohm, ½-W ±10% resistor
R3, R4, R5—5000-ohm subminiature linear control (Mallory MTC53L1 or equiv)
R6—2200-ohm, ½-W ±10% resistor
SW1—spdt wafer switch (Centralab 1460 or equiv)
SW2—spst subminiature push-button switch
M1—0–1 mA dc milliammeter (Lafayette 99F50874 or equiv)
Misc—6″ × 3¾″ × 2″ Bakelite case with aluminum panel; perf board; cigarette-lighter adapter; wire; solder.

# 10

# WINDSHIELD-WASHER
# FLUID WATCHER

Car windshields that are covered by mud spray and slush during winter months and after a summer rain constitute a significant driving hazard. Therefore, windshield washers are an indispensable aid in maintaining safe visibility on crowded highways.

We believe that an indicating system that monitors the washer reservoir to warn you to replenish the windshield-washer fluid before it goes dry is attractive "life insurance" to the driver. The windshield-washer fluid watcher shown in Fig. 10-1 is such a system.

## THE CIRCUIT

Fig. 10-2 shows a very simple circuit for a windshield-washer low-water detector. This circuit relies upon the conduction of a minute current between two conductive probes suspended in the washer-fluid reservoir. Any detergent/antifreeze solution mixed with water makes it a better conductor of electricity. (Ordinarily, there are enough minerals present in most water supplies to guarantee that there will be some current conduction even when ordinary tap water is between the probes.) The "probes" are simply made from a tinned length of 300-ohm tv lead-in wire, with the exposed wire ends located approximately one to two inches from the bottom of

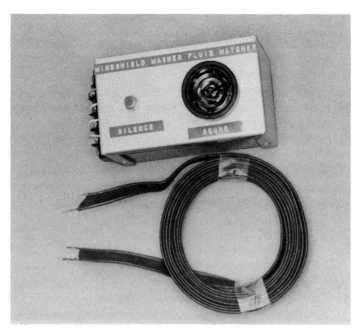

**Fig. 10-1. Windshield-washer fluid watcher.**

the reservoir. One of the probes is connected to R1 and then to +12 volts via the ignition switch. The opposite probe connects directly to the base of a Darlington transistor to minimize the effects of temperature on transistor conduction. Ordinarily, the minute input current to the high-gain Darlington stage maintains the transistor in saturation. Collector current is limited at 60 milliamperes by resistor R2. The saturation voltage at the collector of Q1 (approximately 1 volt) is not sufficient to energize the Sonalert audible signal device. However, if the fluid level falls so that conduction does not take place between the probes, Q1 shuts off and its collector voltage goes more positive. This allows current to energize the Sonalert, which sounds a tone to tell you that the reservoir fluid level is low.

Silicon-controlled rectifier SCR1 and switch S1 give you the ability to silence the Sonalert once its warning has been given. The SCR normally does not conduct until a positive pulse is applied to its gate. This is accomplished with switch S1. When its gate is pulsed, the SCR instantly turns on and latches (remains conducting). This deprives the Sonalert of operating power, since current through R2 is now shunted around the Sonalert, through the SCR to ground. The Sonalert thus remains effectively silenced until the SCR holding current is cut off by breaking the lead to the +12-volt supply.

Power is furnished through the ignition switch contacts, so that the circuit automatically resets every time the switch contacts are opened. However, if the water level is low the next time you start the engine, the Sonalert will sound again, until you silence it with a push of the button. With enough of these gentle reminders, you will take the hint and replenish the washer-fluid supply the next time you gas up!

## CONSTRUCTION

All the components are installed in a 4-inch × 2¼-inch × 2¼-inch aluminum case, which can be mounted at any convenient location under the dash or on the steering column. The parts layout for the windshield-washer fluid watcher is shown in Fig. 10-3. (If you want the fluid watcher located out of sight, switch S1 can be located wherever you choose and the case can be bolted behind the dash.)

The "probe" that goes into the washer reservoir is a length of flat 300-ohm tv twin lead (two wires spaced about ½-inch apart in sturdy plastic insulation). The probe end is cut on

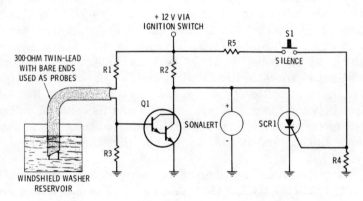

**Fig. 10-2. Circuit for windshield-washer fluid watcher.**

a bias as shown in Fig. 10-4, so that one exposed wire is higher than the other. The exposed ends are tinned to prevent chemical reaction with the washer fluid. The flat ribbon wire is easily slid under the snap-on filler cap if the plastic neck of the reservoir is notched with a file. The wire is then fed back into the driving compartment through one of the firewall holes that are used for existing wiring.

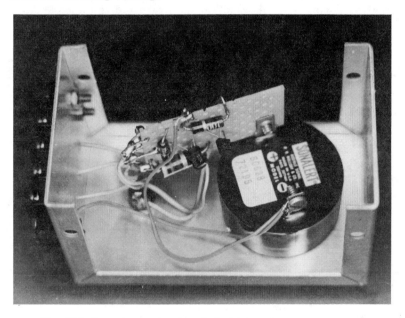

Fig. 10-3. Parts layout for the windshield-washer fluid watcher.

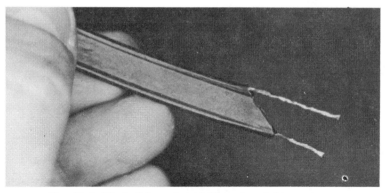

Fig. 10-4. "Probe" for windshield-washer fluid watcher.

It is important that the +12-volt supply line for the windshield-washer fluid watcher come from a point that is controlled by the ignition switch. The radio and heater fan power sources are typical points that you can tie into at the fuse block. Be sure to check with a meter or test lamp to verify that the ignition switch actually removes voltage from the hookup point when the engine is switched off. Otherwise, the unit will remain permanently latched-on the first time you silence it!

**Table 10-1. Windshield-Washer Fluid Watcher Parts List**

Q1—Darlington transistor, type 2N5306 or equiv
R1—10,000-ohm, ½-W ±10% resistor
R2—470-ohm, 1-W ±10% resistor
R3—2.2-megohm, ½-w ±10% resistor
R4—100-ohm, ½-W ±10% resistor
R5—1000-ohm, ½-W ±10% resistor
SCR1—silicon-controlled rectifier (Motorola HEP R1001 or equiv)
Sonalert—P. R. Mallory type SC628
S1—spst normally open push-button switch (Switchcraft type 101 or equiv)
Misc—4" × 2¼" × 2¼" aluminum minibox (Premier PMC-1003 or equiv); length of 300-ohm twin lead; perf board; wire; solder; etc.

# 11

# COURTESY-LIGHT CONTROLLER

How often has this happened to you? You open the car door in the dark of night, the courtesy lights wink on to guide your way into the car, only to plunge you into darkness as you shut the door behind you! When you are burdened by packages or carrying a sleepy child, the dark interior of a car can be downright hostile! Leave the door open, you say? That's all right in summer, as long as rain isn't drenching you. But, in the windy, chilly, drizzly real world, most of us would rather shut out the torments of nature and feel secure within the protective mantle that steel and glass afford. And, part of that secure feeling is a well-lighted car interior.

Add this simple courtesy-light controller (Fig. 11-1) to your car and you can feel at ease entering your vehicle in the dark. As you close the door, the lights remain on, giving you time to place your belongings, buckle your children into their seat belts, and find the ignition lock without scratching up the dash with an ill-directed key. After about one minute, the courtesy lights extinguish. But, by this time, your eyes have become acclimated to the darkness and you are ready to go.

The simple circuit that adds this touch of grace to your car is a three-transistor device that can be installed wherever you have room in your car and access to one of the door-activated courtesy-light switches. The circuit, shown in Fig. 11-2, relies upon the switching logic that is now used in most American cars: the switch that operates the courtesy light simply grounds the lamp return circuit when the door is opened. Closing the door breaks the ground path and extinguishes the light.

The courtesy-light controller circuit is connected *across* the switch—that is, between the lamp return lead and ground— so that when the switch opens (door closed), a path remains for current flow through the courtesy lights, keeping them on. The circuit is designed so that power to the lamps is shut off after a one-minute delay.

## HOW IT WORKS

In operation, npn transistor Q1 is the lamp switching device, with the collector connected to the lamp return lead and the emitter grounded. Silicon-controlled rectifier SCR1 and lamp

Fig. 11-1. Courtesy-light controller.

I1 form a time-delay switching circuit that governs the conduction of Q1.

When the door has been closed for some time (normal condition), capacitor C1 charges to +12 volts, through R1, R2, lamp I1, the emitter-base junction of Q1, and the courtesy lights. However, Q1 is in the nonconducting state, as is SCR1. The gate of SCR1 is grounded through R3, and its cathode is raised above ground by the emitter-base junction of Q1 which functions as a diode.

When the door is opened, C1 is immediately discharged through the door switch. Instantly, the cathode of SCR1 is driven negative, effectively applying a positive-going pulse to the gate. The SCR immediately triggers, commencing current flow through R1, R2, lamp I1, and the emitter-base junction of Q1. This drives Q1 into saturation, supplying a return path for courtesy-lamp current flow when the door is closed again and switch S1 opens.

The SCR latches in the on state and, therefore, the courtesy lamps remain on. Meanwhile, the filament of lamp I1 is heating a built-in bimetallic arm. As time passes, the arm warps and eventually breaks the SCR cathode circuit. At that instant, SCR1 commutates and removes forward bias from transistor Q1. As a result, Q1 ceases to conduct, extinguishing the courtesy lights. As the bimetallic arm of lamp I1 cools, it restores the circuit, but the blocking SCR prevents current flow until

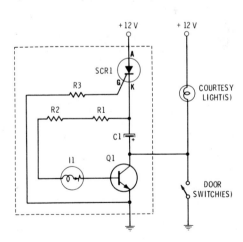

**Fig. 11-2. Schematic diagram of the courtesy-light controller.**

it is once again triggered by a pulse from capacitor C1 as the door opens.

## CONSTRUCTION

Because transistor Q1 is operated as a saturated switch, it dissipates very little heat in the *on* state. Thus, there is no need for a heat sink when load currents are being switched within the free-air dissipating rating of the transistor. (Fortunately, this includes most courtesy-light circuit loads.) As a result, the controller can be housed in any convenient package. Our model fits nicely into a plastic can designed to hold a 35-mm film cartridge. The tightly fitting cap seals-out dust and moisture. All parts can be wired point-to-point, as shown in Fig. 11-3, then tucked inside the can. Three wire leads exit from the can for connection to +12 volts, ground, and the door-switch circuit.

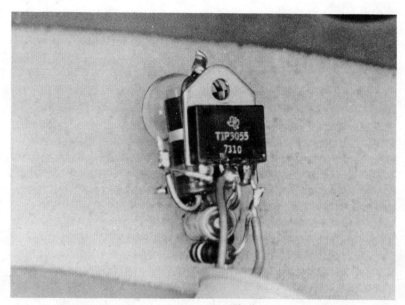

Fig. 11-3. Courtesy-light controller circuit construction.

## USING THE COURTESY-LIGHT CONTROLLER

When all wiring has been correctly completed, open a door after a brief period with the doors closed and note that the courtesy lights come on. Now, close the door. The courtesy lights should remain on, then turn off after about a minute. This cycle should repeat each time the door is closed, then opened, and closed again. If you wish a shorter time delay, reduce the value of resistor R2 slightly.

**Table 11-1. Courtesy-Light Controller Parts List**

C1—10-$\mu$F, 20-V electrolytic capacitor
I1—4.9-V, .3-A flasher lamp (General Electric type 408)
Q1—npn power transistor (Texas Instrument TIP3055 or equiv)
R1, R2—27-ohm, 2-W $\pm$10% resistor
R3—3900-ohm, ½-W $\pm$10% resistor
SCR1—silicon-controlled rectifier (Motorola HEP R1001 or equiv)
Misc—plastic film can with snap-on lid, wire, solder, etc.

# 12

# QUICK-CHECK CIRCUIT TESTER

For a quick diagnosis of car wiring problems, this compact unit is a car-owner's best friend. Since it combines a polarity indicator with a continuity checker, it can answer questions like these: "Is a terminal connected to +12 volts or ground?" "Is the circuit from a given point completed to ground or another point?" "Is the wire, lamp, fuse, or switch 'open'?" "Has insulation been pierced, causing a wire that *should* show +12 volts to be accidentally grounded?"

All these, and more, helpful diagnostic checks can be performed on your car with this shirt-pocket-size instrument (Fig. 12-1). It's not fragile or bulky like a meter, and you don't need outside light to interpret its "readings." Just clip the ground lead to ground and touch the probe to the terminal or point being tested, as shown in Fig. 12-2. A red light-emitting diode (LED) flashes on if the terminal connects to +12 volts, or a green LED switches on to tell you that the point is grounded (or, that there is continuity between probe and clip lead).

## THE CIRCUIT

The schematic of the Quick-Check tester is shown in Fig. 12-3. The circuit relies on external voltage to sense the presence of +12 volts between the probe and clip, or relies on the

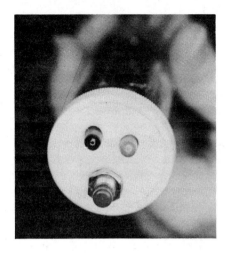

Fig. 12-1. Quick-Check
circuit tester.

internal battery to sense continuity between the probe and
clip.

Transistors Q1 and Q2 comprise a high-gain Darlington
amplifier. LED1 is connected between the collector and emitter
of Q2. Ordinarily, when push-button switch S1 is depressed,
Q1 and Q2 are instantly biased into conduction by current flow
through R1. With transistor Q2 on, the battery voltage is

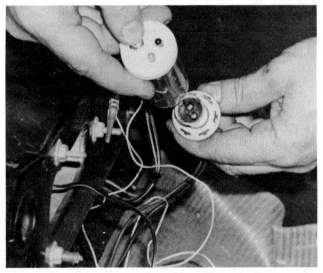

Fig. 12-2. Using the Quick-Check circuit tester.

dropped across R2 so that the only voltage appearing across green LED1 is the saturation voltage of Q2, which is insufficient to excite the LED.

Resistor R3 connects the base of the Q1–Q2 Darlington pair to the probe tip. The clip lead connects to the circuit common or ground, which leads back to the emitter of Q2. If the circuit between the probe and clip is open, LED1 remains off. And, if a positive potential is applied between the probe tip and clip, LED1 continues to be off since the positive input at the probe only serves to drive Q1–Q2 deeper into saturation. However, if the circuit is *completed* between the probe and clip, resistor R3 immediately "pulls down" the voltage at the base of Q1–Q2 so that insufficient current can flow to turn the Darlington pair on. Immediately, the collector voltage of Q2 rises, exciting LED1 into conduction. Similarly, if a sufficiently negative voltage appears between the probe and clip, Q1 and Q2 are biased off and LED1 illuminates.

Transistor Q3 controls operation of the red positive-voltage detector, LED2. It is responsive only to the presence of a voltage greater than +6 volts, applied between the probe and the ground clip. This voltage supplies forward bias to Q3 through resistor R4 and provides collector voltage through resistor R5 and LED2. With the probe and clip open or shorted, no supply voltage is provided and LED2 is off. Furthermore, a negative voltage between the probe and clip reverse-biases LED2 and Q3 so that the LED remains off. Thus, only if the probe is applied to a wire or terminal that has a positive voltage with respect to ground (clip) does transistor Q3 conduct and turn

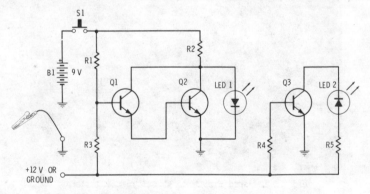

Fig. 12-3. Schematic of the Quick-Check circuit tester.

on LED2. This checker is a reliable detector of the presence of voltage at a point, or of the presence of a path from the probe to the clip lead (ground, if you choose).

Resistors R1, R3, and R4 limit current flow in the base-emitter junctions of transistors Q1, Q2, and Q3 to a safe value. Resistors R2 and R5 limit the maximum current flow to LED1 and LED2 to about 20 milliamperes, a current that yields the best battery life and maximum brightness of the light-emitting diodes. The push-button switch saves the battery when the checker is not in use.

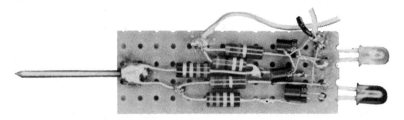

Fig. 12-4. Component side of circuit board.

## CONSTRUCTION

Compactness and a package that is small enough to fit into your hand are features of the checker's design. But, of course,

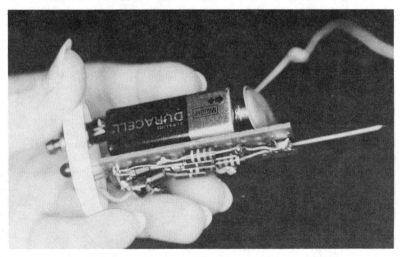

Fig. 12-5. Complete assembly removed from the bottle.

you can vary the packaging to suit your needs and the availability of parts.

The authors' version is packaged in a 1¼-inch diameter × 2⅞-inch long plastic pill bottle with a snap-on top. The empty bottle easily accommodates a 9-volt battery, the two LEDs, transistors, resistors, and switch. The probe tip is a 1¼-inch finishing nail. (If you want an insulation-piercing probe, sharpen the tip to a fine point on a bench grinder.) The components nestle snugly inside the bottle. The LEDs and switch mount on the snap-on cap. Figs. 12-4 and 12-5 show the parts layout in detail.

### USING THE CHECKER

Clip the ground-lead wire to one end of the car circuit to be checked (ground to chassis, for example) and use the probe to touch significant points in the rest of the circuit, pressing switch S1 as you do so. Where there is a positive voltage, the red LED will light; where there is a ground, the green LED will light. Neither LED will light with an open circuit. A bit of practice will make you a whiz at checking out auto electrical circuits with this easy-to-use helper.

### Table 12-1. Quick-Check Circuit Tester Parts List

```
B1—9-V battery (Mallory MN1604 or equiv)
LED1—green light-emitting diode (Lafayette 32-06349 or equiv)
LED2—red light-emitting diode (Lafayette 32-06331 or equiv)
Q1, Q2, Q3—npn silicon transistor, type 2N2926 or equiv
R1—100,000-ohm, ½-W ±10% resistor
R2, R5—150-ohm, ½-W ±10% resistor
R3, R4—15,000-ohm, ½-W ±10% resistor
S1—miniature normally open push-button switch
Misc—2⅞″ × 1¼″ diameter plastic pill bottle; 2½″ × ⅞″ perf board;
    battery snap terminals; ground lead with alligator clip; wire; solder;
    etc.
```

# 13

# TURN-SIGNAL ALERT

You flick the turn-signal lever as you commence a lane change or shallow turn. The lever latches and the turn-signal lights blink obediently, flashing a warning to vehicles ahead and behind that you are about to make your move. It's a nice day for driving—the sun is shining brightly, the window is down and the radio is turned up. Result? The turn signals keep blinking long after your turn, because the steering wheel did not turn far enough to unlatch the turn-signal lever and you neither saw the indicator light, nor heard the soft clicking of the flasher.

This seemingly innocuous occurrence can have some grisly consequences. It leaves drivers of other cars guessing about your intentions and may lead to an accident under certain conditions.

The simple Turn-Signal Alert shown in Fig. 13-1 won't let that happen to you. Flip the lever to signal a turn and the circuit within the Alert is activated. It waits about a minute, giving you ample time to complete your turn or lane change; then it sounds off with a tone that pulses at the turn-signal flash rate to let you know that the lights are still blinking. Of course, if the turn-signal lever has been moved back to neutral (either manually or automatically), the circuit instantly resets until the next time the signals are switched on.

The pulsing tone is produced by a Sonalert (Fig. 13-2), a solid-state sounder that unleashes a distinctive 2500-Hz note

Fig. 13-1. The Turn-Signal Alert.

that is easily heard through the din of traffic or over the noise of "hard rock."

## HOW IT WORKS

The turn-signal circuit used in most present-day cars is shown in simplified form at the top of Fig. 13-3. The directional switch is basically a single-pole, double-throw switch, and its arm is supplied with 12 volts through a flasher. The

Fig. 13-2. The Sonalert.

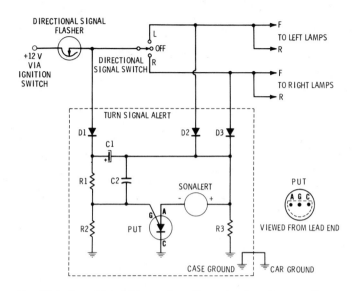

**Fig. 13-3. Turn-Signal Alert schematic and external connections.**

flasher contains a bimetallic strip that closes with a fixed contact when the circuit is open and no current is flowing. Moving the switch to either position applies the load to the flasher consisting of either the left or right set of signal lamps. The rush of current through the load heats the bimetallic strip, and it snaps to an open but unstable state, breaking the circuit. As the strip cools, it snaps closed again, and the cycle repeats until the turn-signal switch is moved to the neutral position, breaking the circuit to the lamps.

The Turn-Signal Alert is tied into the circuit at three points: diode D1 connects to the flasher; diodes D2 and D3 connect to the wires connected respectively to the left and right turn-signal lamps.

The circuit draws no current when the ignition switch is off, and draws only a few microamperes in its sensing state when the ignition switch is on. In the latter state, +12 volts is applied through the closed flasher contacts across resistors R1 and R2, causing capacitor C1 to charge through R3. As long as the turn-signal switch is in the neutral (open-circuit) position, nothing happens. However, when that switch is moved to either the left or right signal position, +12 volts is applied through either diode D2 or D3, and the Sonalert to the anode of programmable unijunction transistor PUT1.

PUT1 is in the nonconducting state because its gate is more positive than its anode. In order to conduct, the gate must be at least 0.6 volt *below* the anode potential. At the instant that the turn-signal switch is closed, +12 volts is applied across resistor R3, and this potential appears in series with the charge stored on capacitor C1. As a result, the voltage appearing across R1 and R2 is now +24 volts, making the gate *very* positive with respect to the anode. Capacitor C2 helps to immunize the gate circuit against transients during this period.

However, as the flasher cycles, capacitor C1 commences to discharge through R1, R2, and R3 and to recharge *in the opposite polarity*, through diode D2 or D3. Gradually, the gate voltage falls until a point is reached where the capacitor recharge cycle has depressed the gate voltage below the anode voltage. At this point, the PUT triggers on and latches, supplying a ground path for the Sonalert. A pulsed tone now occurs each time the flasher circuit supplies +12 volts to the turn-signal lamps. If the turn-signal switch is moved to neutral, the PUT is deprived of holding current and the device blocks. Almost instantly, C1 recharges in the polarity to block the PUT and the circuit resets, awaiting closure of the turn-signal switch to commence a new timing period.

## CONSTRUCTION

The Turn-Signal Alert is housed in a miniature aluminum case, as shown in Fig. 13-4. The Sonalert mounts to the larger

Fig. 13-4. Internal view of the Turn-Signal Alert.

flat surface of one case half, and a four-terminal strip is secured to the top of that case half. All connections to the turn-signal circuit and ground are made at the screw terminals.

The PUT and the few circuit components are wired point to point, with the Sonalert terminals used as mechanical supports. If you wish, a perf-board construction method can be used, but the simplicity of the circuit and the light weight of its components make this unnecessary. Be sure to observe correct polarity of diodes D1, D2, and D3, and electrolytic capacitor C1.

## INSTALLATION AND CHECKOUT

Mount the assembled unit at any convenient point under the dash or along the sidewall where it will not be easily kicked and will not interfere with the accelerator and brake pedals. Run wire leads to the flasher and to the separate feed wires for the left and right turn-signal lamps. (If you have trouble finding the correct wires, check the color of the wires leading through the engine compartment to the front turn-signal lamps or consult your car's shop manual.) Be sure to make a good ground connection to the car body.

When the hookup is complete, turn the ignition switch on and place the turn-signal lever in the left or right position. In about a minute, the Sonalert's tone will be heard, pulsing on and off with the turn-signal lamps. Flip the turn-signal switch to neutral and note that the Sonalert is silenced; then, move the switch to the opposite position for another timing cycle. The action should be the same.

If you find yourself trapped in traffic or at a long light, while signalling a turn, just move the turn-signal lever to neutral for an instant to silence and reset the Alert. And, the first time you hear its warning note when you thought the turn signals were off, we are sure you will agree that the few minutes spent in building the Turn-Signal Alert were well worth the effort.

## Table 13-1. Turn-Signal Alert Parts List

C1—25-$\mu$F, 25-V dc electrolytic capacitor
C2—.01-$\mu$F, 200-V dc disc or Mylar capacitor
D1, D2, D3—general-purpose silicon diode (Motorola HEP R0050 or equiv)
PUT1—programmable unijunction transistor (General Electric GE-X17 or equiv)
R1—470,000-ohm, ½-W ±10% resistor
R2—2.2-megohm, ½-W ±10% resistor
R3—2700-ohm, ½-W ±10% resistor
Sonalert—P. R. Mallory type SC628
Misc—4″ × 2¼″ × 2¼″ aluminum minibox (Bud CU-2103A or equiv); 4-terminal screw-type terminal strip; wire; solder; etc.